REFRACTIONS: SCENES

ALSO BY YVETTE NOLAN

Annie Mae's Movement
Medicine Shows: Indigenous Performance Culture
Performing Indigeneity (edited with Ric Knowles)
Refractions: Solo (edited with Donna-Michelle St. Bernard)
The Unplugging

ALSO BY DONNA-MICHELLE ST. BERNARD

Cake
Gas Girls
Indian Act: Residential School Plays (editor)
A Man A Fish
Refractions: Solo (edited with Yvette Nolan)
Sound of the Beast

REFRACTIONS: SCENES

**EDITED BY YVETTE NOLAN AND
DONNA-MICHELLE ST. BERNARD**

PLAYWRIGHTS CANADA PRESS
TORONTO

LIBRARY AND ARCHIVES CANADA CATALOGUING IN PUBLICATION
Title: Refractions : scenes / edited by Yvette Nolan, Donna-Michelle St. Bernard.
Other titles: Refractions (2020)
Names: Nolan, Yvette, editor. | St. Bernard, Donna-Michelle, editor.
Description: First edition.
Identifiers: Canadiana 20200377957 | ISBN 9781770919624 (softcover)
Subjects: LCSH: Monologues, Canadian. | LCSH: Canadian drama—21st century.
 | CSH: Monologues, Canadian (English) | CSH: Canadian drama (English)
 —21st century.
Classification: LCC PS8309.M6 R44 2020 | DDC c812/.04508—dc23

Playwrights Canada Press operates on Mississaugas of the Credit, Wendat, Anishinaabe, Métis, and Haudenosaunee land. It always was and always will be Indigenous land.

We acknowledge the financial support of the Canada Council for the Arts—which last year invested $153 million to bring the arts to Canadians throughout the country—the Ontario Arts Council (OAC), Ontario Creates, and the Government of Canada for our publishing activities.

 Canada Council for the Arts / Conseil des arts du Canada

 ONTARIO ARTS COUNCIL / CONSEIL DES ARTS DE L'ONTARIO / an Ontario government agency / un organisme du gouvernement de l'Ontario

 Canadä

 ONTARIO CREATES | ONTARIO CRÉATIF

For Daniel David Moses
And George Boyd
In whose footsteps we walk

CONTENTS

SIX DIRECTIONS THAT TELL US WHERE WE ARE

HOW DO WE KNOW WHERE WE ARE?

In Indigenous country, we talk about six directions: north, south, east, west, above, and below. You, me, we are at the crossroads of those directions. We are here.

BUT WHERE IS HERE?

This is the place we move forward from, and in which a part of us is left behind or rooted. These plays we have chosen, they tell us where we are too, but our directions are both geographic and abstract. These playwrights grapple with living on this land we currently call Canada with an awareness of all that it stands on, stands for, stands in relation to.

In the monologue collection *Refractions: Solo* we considered how splitting light through a prism offers a fuller vision. Once again we aim to illuminate the vast and diverse landscape of contemporary Canadian theatre, but in *Scenes* we are always in relation to others. Here we find ourselves in refracted territories, familiar and unknown.

Some of those territories are physical, some are landscapes of the heart or mind.

INWARD

Donna-Michelle likes to start with a piece by a First Nation writer, but we thought to begin this collection with George Boyd's *Consecrated Ground* because he captures both the connection to and the grief of being uprooted from the land. In Daniel David Moses's *Brébeuf's Ghost*, another community flees for its life. In *REDPATCH*, a young man from this land fights on someone else's territory for a foreign set of values.

OUTWARD

Sometimes what we know of this land is forged in other places, by a massacre in Nanking, a *coup d'état* in Chile, in a Russian freighter picking up stowaways in the Strait of Gibraltar, in a coal truck smuggling women in newly divided Hindustan.

SELF

Tensions born of the disparity between internal compasses and external expectations result in acts ranging from the courageous to the unconscionable. In these scenes identity is often both the battlefield and the casualty.

PAST

These writers contend with the past, whether through encounters with their ancestors, as in Mike Czuba's *Reprise*, or with the ideas of who we are that have been cemented in stories we have come to believe, as in Audrey Dwyer's *Calpurnia*. Leonard Linklater unearths not just the injustice of early encounters between newcomers and First Nations, but the reasons why things went so badly wrong so quickly.

PRESENT

"There is no such thing as bad luck! Not here. Not in Canada. You make your own luck," Michaela di Cesare's Anthony says in *Successions*. The characters in these excerpts attempt to make their own luck, whether that's by undergoing a makeover so extreme that you no longer fit into your life, as in Evan Tsitsias's *Aftershock*, or breaking into a mansion to hold the party to end all parties in Colleen Murphy's *I Hope My Heart Burns First*.

FUTURE

Where will we end up if we keep going like this? Marie Clements, Frances Koncan, and Ciarán Myers trace a line from where we are to an imagined eventual, extrapolating from our complicity to our comeuppance. Yet each offers hope in unlikely acts of resistance, subversion, survival.

We hope that you find yourself somewhere in these pages, and that you seek out the plays excerpted here so that you can lose yourself in the full narrative these thirty-six creators have crafted. Here are six directions. And here we are.

—YN & DM

INWARD

GEORGE BOYD
CONSECRATED GROUND

George Elroy Boyd was a highly acclaimed Nova Scotian playwright and journalist. His plays have been produced by Neptune Theatre, Eastern Front Theatre, Obsidian Theatre, and the CBC. The founder of the Canadian Black Theatre Society, Boyd was nominated for a Governor General's Literary Award for his play *Consecrated Ground* (2000), and *Gideon's Blues* has been adapted into a film, which was released in the winter of 2004. He passed away in July 2020.

In *Consecrated Ground*, George Boyd retells the struggle of Africville's residents to save their homes and their dignity. With tremendous wit and gravity, Boyd takes us back to Africville on the verge of extinction, making us a gift of characters believable in their vulnerabilities, their courage, and their outrage.

Consecrated Ground was first performed at the Sir James Dunn Theatre, Halifax, on Friday, January 14, 1999, under the auspices of Eastern Front Theatre.

* * *

All save the REVEREND *have gathered at the church.*

JIMMY: W-W-What you think the-the-the—

GROOVEY: "The Reverend wants?!" Spit it out, fool, 'cause Groovey Peters got her no patience today.

SARAH: (*admonishing*) Groovey! Now what I tell you?

CLARICE: Whatcha think, Aunt Sarah?

SARAH: Well, the last time Sarah been at a "family meeting"—

WILLEM: I ain't from Africville. What do that mean, Leasey? "Family meetin'"?

JIMMY: It-it-it—

SARAH: Yes we is. We all family, son, and we all in God's church.

CLARICE: It means all of us folk here gets together, honey. And just *us* folks. We ah . . . (*chuckles*) manage to avoid invitin' the whites.

SARAH: And it mean somethin' import be up. We don't call a family meetin' to talk, foolishin's.

Beat.

Hear that, Groovey?

GROOVEY: Now Groovey Peters be sittin' right here, Aunt Sarah.

The REVEREND *enters, removing his coat, and goes to the pulpit.*

REVEREND MINER: Now I'm not gonna preach to y'all—

He gets down and stands on the floor, looking at them.

—I'm not gonna pontificate, I'm gonna elucidate . . .

GROOVEY: Hell-oh!

SARAH: Groovey! Now what I tell ya?!

CLARICE: Go ahead, Reverend.

REVEREND MINER: Now I know ya all seen that white man around here a lot.

JIMMY: Oh Lawd.

REVEREND MINER: We all seen him, we know that. Well he's not here 'cause he likes the view—

JIMMY: He's here on ba-ba-ba-ba-ba-ba-ba-ba—

GROOVEY: Now the damned fool sound like a sheep!

SARAH: Groovey!

JIMMY:—business!

SARAH: What kind of business, Reverend?

REVEREND MINER: City business. He's here because he's been instructed by his bosses—the city—to buy your land.

CLARICE: Well we ain't sellin'!

WILLEM: Leasey, will you *listen* to Reverend Miner?

CLARICE, holding Tully, stands and gathers her purse.

CLARICE: No, let's go home, Willem. 'Cause we ain't sellin', so this ain't none of our business.

REVEREND MINER: I think you should stay, Leasey. Really.

WILLEM: I wanna hear what the Reverend's gotta say. If it affects Africville—I wanna hear.

Reluctantly CLARICE sits.

REVEREND MINER: Like I was saying, this man—this Clancy—he's here on official city business. Now they're going to develop this land and they're making financial offers. Offering those with families a place in Uniacke Square.

JIMMY: The-the-the projects!

CLARICE: Then they gotta pay us.

REVEREND MINER: Yes. A fair price—the city assures me. Now think of this: you all be close by. You'll have all the amenities the white folks have—water and plumbing. You'll be closer to grocery stores, hospitals, and schools. *And*—we'll have the church right here in Africville.

SARAH: Hallelujah!

CLARICE: *(standing)* Now when the city gonna be fair to niggers? Never have, never will be, I say.

(to WILLEM) I tol' ya this ain't got nothing to do with us, Willem. We ain't sellin'. Now c'mon.

CLARICE exits with Tully. WILLEM stays.

GROOVEY: Rev'rund Miner?

REVEREND MINER: Yes, Groovey?

GROOVEY: You been talkin' to de city?

REVEREND MINER: I have.

GROOVEY: And you never told us?

REVEREND MINER: The meetings were confidential. And I was forced to keep my mouth shut or I probably would not have been invited. We wouldn't even possess this much information. Now keeping the church was a struggle—but that's the great thing. We all know what the church means to coloured folk: it's our monument to those who died on the middle passage—every spirit that lies on the bottom of the Atlantic.

ALL: *(variously)* Amen . . . That's right . . . Uh huh . . . *(etc.)*

REVEREND MINER: The church embodies all that we do: it's where we baptize our young, and not-so-young. Where we get hope, when hope doesn't appear to be on the horizon. Where we mourn and get strength for the loss of a loved one. The church, as you all know, is a living monument. A testament to a race or Black people: a proud, hard-working, and loving people. Our divine power and spirituality— all of our mothers. It is the very cement which our community was founded upon. Our sustenance when we're weak—

SARAH: Yes, Lord.

REVEREND MINER: Our warmth when we are cold. Our very essence itself.

SARAH: Praise God.

REVEREND MINER: So just because we live down the street—a little way from here—Africville will never die. In this church, our soul shall live.

GROOVEY: You said you wasn't gonna preach!!

SARAH: (*standing up*) That was a *great* sermon and such, Reverend. Fancy words and all. But lemme tell you this: it's well known that if you lay down with dogs, you come up with fleas.

She sits.

ALL: (*variously*) Go on, Aunt Sarah! I hear ya! (*etc.*)

REVEREND MINER: Africville will not be lost—you'll all be neighbours in the city.

JIMMY: G-g-g-good! Then we can all m-m-m-move together!

REVEREND MINER: Where there will be no bulldozers. No dumps. No abattoir stench, and above all—no rats.

JIMMY: They-they-they gittin' bigger than the c-c-c-cats, Reverend—

GROOVEY: So what do we do now, mun?

REVEREND MINER: Go home—

All save REVEREND MINER start to exit.

Wait for this white man, this Mr. Clancy, to approach you with an offer. If you decide to move, he assures me everything will be handled in an orderly fashion.

GROOVEY: Good! *(standing)* What he look like, honey?

SARAH: Groovey, git your mind out the—

She grabs GROOVEY's arm.

—c'mon, girl.

The congregation exits. The REVEREND stands alone. Blackout.

DANIEL DAVID MOSES
BRÉBEUF'S GHOST

Daniel David Moses was "a coroner of the theatre who slices open the human heart to reveal the fear, hatred, and love that have eaten away at it. His dark play . . . can leave its audience shaking with emotion" (Kate Taylor, *The Globe and Mail*, about *The Indian Medicine Shows*). Moses, a Delaware from the Six Nations lands on the Grand River, lived in Toronto, where he wrote, and in Kingston, where he taught in the Department of Drama at Queen's University. He passed away in July 2020.

1649 brings bad news to Lake Nipissing—the Iroquois are on the war-path, killing Christians at Sainte Marie. Guess who's going to be next? The shaman's worried about cannibals, the Black Robe about the fires of hell—worlds collide in this rich and strange epic of early Canada.

Brébeuf's Ghost was first performed at Essex Hall Theatre, University of Windsor, on May 29, 1996, in a production by the author and the Department of English and the School of Dramatic Art of the Faculty of Arts at the University of Windsor.

* * *

The full moon high in the sky. The sandy landing on the La Vase River shore below the village. Four canoes almost packed and ready for departure lie at the edge of the sand. FLOOD *Woman sits in* IRON *Man's canoe, rocking the restless baby boy North Star.* HAIL *Stone Woman and* THISTLE *stand nearby on the sand,* HAIL *Stone Woman with a paddle in her hand.*

FLOOD: *(singing a lullaby)* Hush, now, hush, baby boy.
Go to sleep, deep as fish
Go to sleep. Hush, now, hush,
Stars close their eyes in the lake.

THISTLE: She'll be back soon.

HAIL: Black Star's making medicine to find her.

THISTLE: She'll be back. We don't need his help. Father Noel, he's praying for her.

HAIL: Well we can't wait. Not now.

THISTLE: I've been praying too.

HAIL: One of the men will find her.

THISTLE: I've been trying to pray. I should have made her talk to Father Noel.

THISTLE begins to cry.

HAIL: Someone will find her. We'll see you soon.

Baby boy North Star whines.

THISTLE: I'm going to go pray some more with the Father.

THISTLE exits toward the village.

HAIL: Quiet him. Someone's coming.

FLOOD: Hush, now, hush baby boy . . .

CLOUD: *(entering along the beach)* Where's your husband, woman?

HAIL: Your wife's with the Black Robe.

CLOUD: What are you talking about?

HAIL: My husband's ready to go. We have to go now.

CLOUD: Has my daughter come back? We'll wait for her.

HAIL: No, we can't. My husband was down to the village at the point. He heard about Iroquois hunting down in the narrows into the bay.

IRON Man enters, carrying the crippled Star LILY.

CLOUD: We'll wait.

HAIL: We can't. Not with them that close.

IRON Man puts Star LILY down in the canoe beside FLOOD Woman.

CLOUD: This woman of yours, she says you want to leave.

IRON: The families at the point, they've already left. Their young men are singing their war songs. We'll go on ahead, prepare the hiding place.

CLOUD: What about my daughter?

HAIL: She's a stupid girl, chasing after that old man's son.

CLOUD: Can't you keep your woman quiet!

IRON: Get in the canoe.

IRON Man takes the paddle from HAIL Stone Woman.

HAIL: Does he want us all to die on account of her? She's as good as dead by now.

IRON: Get in!

He slaps her butt with the paddle.

HAIL Stone Woman gets in the canoe.

CLOUD: You're taking all that meat?

IRON: I have to look after my own woman.

CLOUD: Wait till the others come back. Maybe one of them has found her.

LILY: Bear and the Frenchman came back already.

CLOUD: She wasn't in the east?

IRON: And you saw no sign north of here.

CLOUD: I found an Iroquois canoe. I tore the skin off it.

HAIL: They've got her for sure.

CLOUD: And Black Star?

LILY: He's singing. But he hasn't seen her.

FLOOD: Singing and singing.

LILY: He can't see her for the hunger.

FLOOD: Hush, now, hush, baby . . .

LILY: Winter's going to be bad.

HAIL: You're shivering.

LILY: The hunger's coming this way.

HAIL: Put the blanket on.

IRON: It'll be too light if we wait.

CLOUD: You're right.

IRON: We can't travel fast.

CLOUD: Go on then.

IRON Man pushes his canoe out into the lake.

HAIL: Husband, you know what they do to young women. Tell him I'm sorry.

Clouds cover the moon.

IRON: My wife has a big mouth. She—

CLOUD: Go on!

IRON Man jumps into his canoe with HAIL Stone Woman, FLOOD Woman, and North Star. Fire CLOUD pushes it out of the shallows into an exit.

FLOOD: Hush, now, hush, baby boy. Go to sleep, deep as fish . . .

VOICE: *(off)* Father! Father!

CLOUD: Down here, boy. Here!

Thunder VOICE enters, pushing PIERRE, arms bound behind his back, ahead of him.

VOICE: My sister's alive, Father.

CLOUD: What? Where is she?

PIERRE: Please, I'm hungry and cold.

CLOUD: What's he saying? Does he know where she is?

VOICE: I think so, Father. I heard my sister's voice. But I couldn't find her.

CLOUD: It's all rocks over there.

VOICE: I couldn't find her trail.

Black STAR and BEAR enter.

PIERRE: Build me a fire tonight.

VOICE: But then I caught this one running out of the trees.

PIERRE: Please?

STAR: Put him down. Be careful. Are the thongs tight?

VOICE: I took him back into the rocks. There was a dead Huron there.

CLOUD: He kill him?

VOICE: I don't think so. He was afraid like a dog.

STAR: Did you burn the body? These are the cannibals I told you about.

VOICE: Are you sure?

STAR: A young Black Robe and a Huron.

CLOUD: He talks like the Black Robe.

VOICE: Does he know where she is?

PIERRE: A little mouse?

STAR: He's seen someone alive.

CLOUD: Look at the way he stares.

BEAR: Where's the body?

VOICE: Other side of the swamp.

STAR: Keep him tied tight.

VOICE: He doesn't look like a cannibal.

CLOUD: You've never seen one before.

Black STAR and BEAR exit.

CLOUD: Come on, you, on your feet.

VOICE: The Black Robe will make you tell us where she is.

Thunder VOICE pulls PIERRE to his feet and they exit, following Fire CLOUD.

LISA CODRINGTON
UP THE GARDEN PATH

Lisa Codrington is a Toronto-based actor and writer. Her writing has been produced in Toronto, Niagara-on-the-Lake, Winnipeg, and Barbados, and has been published by Playwrights Canada Press, McGraw-Hill Ryerson, and in *Canadian Theatre Review*. Select writing credits include *The Aftermath*, *The Colony*, *The Adventures of the Black Girl in Her Search for God*, and *Cast Iron*, which was shortlisted for the Governor General's Literary Award for Drama. Lisa is a recipient of the Carol Bolt Award for *Up the Garden Path* and the K.M. Hunter Artist Award. She has been playwright-in-residence at a number of theatres, including Canadian Stage, Nightwood Theatre, the Blyth Festival, and the Shaw Festival.

In *Up the Garden Path*, Rosa, a young Barbadian seamstress, offers to pose as her brother to go to the Niagara Region in Ontario to work. There, she meets an aspiring actress obsessed with Joan of Arc, the ghost of a Black Loyalist soldier who wants to die, and a boss who can't keep the starlings away from his failing vineyard. Finding it impossible to ignore their demands, but not wanting to be found out and sent home, Rosa has to stop and figure out what she really wants instead of what everyone around her needs.

Up the Garden Path was first performed at Theatre Passe Muraille, Toronto, on March 23, 2016, in a production by Obsidian Theatre.

* * *

Tuesday morning.

ALMA's broken-down board house.

De sun shinin' bright, but it ain't got de place suh hot yet.

EDMUND stands uncomfortably in a half-altered suit. He eats turnover while ROSA tries not to juk he wit' straight pins. ALMA and AMELIA hover.

EDMUND: We have some land in DE back and / I tend tuh—

AMELIA: No no no. "We have some LAND in de back and I TEND tuh it!"

EDMUND: We have SOME land in de back / and I tend—

AMELIA: We have some LAND in de back and I TEND tuh it!

EDMUND: We have some land IN de BACK and I tend TUH it!

Pause.

AMELIA: Just keep practisin' and yuh be fine.

ALMA: Fine what! If de boy can't even talk 'bout tendin' land, how de hell he gine get de damn seeds plant when he overseas?

EDMUND: *(quietly)* We have some LAND / in de BACK and I tend tuh IT.

AMELIA: He ain't gotta plant; he just gotta pick de fruit when it ripe.

ALMA: Yuh gotta plant tuh have somet'ing tuh pick.

AMELIA: I tell yuh, it gine be done plant by de time he reach de place.

ALMA: How you know?

EDMUND: (*a little louder*) WE have SOME land / in de back and I tend TUH it.

AMELIA: I done quarrellin', 'cause you ain't know a damn t'ing 'bout food but how tuh eat it.

ALMA: Why should I hurt my hand if Edie-muh-sweetie / can just go up de street tuh Ms. Clarke's shop an—

AMELIA sucks her teeth.

AMELIA: Yuh should stop callin' he dat.

ALMA: Why?

AMELIA: It mek he soft.

EDMUND: (*even louder*) WE have some / land in de back AND I TEND tuh it.

ALMA: (*to AMELIA*) How was I supposed tuh mek he hard all on my own?

AMELIA: Yuh shoulda gone wit' de Forde guy; he did like you bad.

ALMA: He have a funny eye.

AMELIA: Wha' yuh got tuh look at he suh hard fuh? A man is a man! Yuh lucky yuh get one—

EDMUND: (*full blast*) WE HAVE SOME LAND IN DE BACK AND I TEND TUH IT!

AMELIA: Lawrd Gawd, yuh tryin' tuh give we heart attack!

EDMUND: Sorry, Auntie.

ROSA: Stand still. I nearly juk yuh.

AMELIA: Yuh carry on like dat at yuh interview and yuh can forget about overseas—dem will tek yuh straight tuh de madhouse!

ALMA: Let de boy practise nuh!

AMELIA: I am tryin' tuh help he—

ALMA: Well lower down yuh voice den. Wit' de way YOU is carry on, it no wonder yuh ain't NEVER get nuh man.

(*to EDMUND*) Go on, Edie.

EDMUND: (*quietly*) Land land, we have SOOOME / LAAAAND . . .

AMELIA: Yuh forget Alton who live up top de hill?

ALMA: Who?

AMELIA: My man dat guh 'long tuh England.

ALMA: Oh, Alton dat lef' yuh tail.

AMELIA: (*to ROSA*) He was tuh send fuh muh but—

ALMA: (*to* ROSA) Up till now she ain't never hear from de man.

EDMUND: (*quietly*) Weeee haaaaave / SOME—

AMELIA: (*to* ROSA) It dat pale-face postman. He vex 'cause I turn he down. / Suh what he gone and do? Strip up alla Alton letters! / I gine confront he tomorrow. / And den I gine write tuh Alton and mek my way tuh England.

EDMUND: (*quietly*) We we WEEEE HAAAAVE . . .

(*quietly*) We HAVE some . . .

(*quietly*) SOME SOME, we have . . .

    ALMA *dies wit' de laugh.*

AMELIA: (*to* ROSA) T'ink you could mek me a dress fuh de trip?

ROSA: Yes.

AMELIA: Good. If it fit nice yuh can mek my weddin' dress.

EDMUND: (*quietly*) Land, / la la la la . . .

ALMA: (*to* AMELIA) Yuh gine invite de queen tuh de weddin' too?

AMELIA: I ain't want she turnup face and small small nose at my special day.

ALMA: Yuh get hang fuh dat, yuh hear.

AMELIA: We is an independent nation now. I can say what I want.

ALMA: All right den, but if yuh gine all de way tuh England to meet up wit' you man ALTON, in you PRETTY PRETTY dress for you BIG BIG day, yuh might as well guh down tuh de palace and have some tea wit' de queen TOO, / 'cause DE TWO A WE KNOW DAT AIN'T NEVER—

AMELIA: I gine mek yuh see de QUEEN right now, 'CAUSE I GINE GIVE YUH SOME LICKS / DAT GINE LEF' YUH RASS'OLE—

ALMA sings "God Save the Queen" until EDMUND cries out.

ALMA: God save our gracious Queen!
Long live our noble Queen! /
God save de Queen!
Send her victorious,
Happy and glorious
Long to reign over—

AMELIA sings the Barbadian national anthem, "In Plenty and In Time of Need," until EDMUND cries out.

AMELIA: In plenty and in time of need
When dis fair land was young
Our brave forefadders sowed de seed
From which our pride is—

ROSA juks EDMUND in the leg with a pin and he cries out, cutting off ALMA and AMELIA's singing / fighting.

EDMUND: AYE!

ROSA: I tell yuh tuh stand still.

EDMUND rubs his leg.

ALMA: *(gasps)* Lawrd Gawd she draw blood!

ROSA: Sorry.

ALMA: Come and sit, Edie. Before yuh fall down of bad feels.

AMELIA: We ain't got time fuh dis. Rosa need tuh finish—

ALMA: *(to ROSA)* Dis you plan? Bring alla you dirty pins up in here, play you mekin' a suit, den juk alla we in de foot, t'row we bodies in de gully and lef' we fuh dead?

AMELIA: She barely juk he.

ALMA: Auntie Bea barely get juk in she foot, but it pain she suh bad dat de doctor had tuh come and cut it off. But he cut off de wrong one, suh den he have tuh do de NEXT one, so now BOT' a she foot cut off. Come, Edie. Let we get dat foot in some Epsom salts—

EDMUND: I fine. Let we just finish suh I can tek dis damn t'ing off.

ALMA:

> *EDMUND goes back to reciting "I have some land in de back and I tend tuh it" and* ROSA *goes back to trying not to juk he wit' straight pins.*

RAES CALVERT AND SEAN HARRIS OLIVER
REDPATCH

Raes Calvert is a Métis theatre artist who lives and works in
Vancouver. As a performer he has toured nationally and inter-
nationally with such companies as Axis Theatre, Green Thumb
Theatre, Manitoba Theatre for Young People, Neworld Theatre, and
Presentation House Theatre. After graduating from Studio 58 at
Langara College in 2010, he and colleague Sean Harris Oliver began
Hardline Productions. Raes is a three-time Jessie Richardson Theatre
Award nominee and one-time recipient. He is also a recipient of the
REVEAL Indigenous Art Award from the Hnatyshyn Foundation.

Sean Harris Oliver is a Governor General's Literary Award–nom-
inated playwright (*The Fighting Season*, 2019), screenwriter, and
director. His short play *Eight Seconds* was originally staged at
Vancouver's Pull Festival before going on to be produced in New
York, Massachusetts, and Florida. His first full-length play, *Bright
Blue Future*, was a finalist for the Theatre BC Playwriting Competition
and was produced by Hardline Productions. Sean is a graduate of
Studio 58.

Between 1914 and 1918 over four thousand First Nations soldiers
volunteered to fight and die for Canada in the First World War. Set
in both Canada and the battlefields of France, *REDPATCH* follows
the experiences of a young Métis solider from the Nuu-chah-nulth
nation of Vancouver Island who volunteers to fight for Canada in the
First World War and endures the horrors of war.

REDPATCH was first performed at Presentation House Theatre,
Vancouver, on March 29, 2017, in a production by Hardline Productions.

* * *

Present. Spring 1915 through fall 1916.

The steady beat of a drum.

HALF-BLOOD: The battle of Ypres gave us a reputation.

DICKEY: A reputation as warriors, Winnifred.

BAM-BAM: The Brits throw us into battle after battle. BAM! BAM!

DICKEY: *Shock troopers.* That's what they're calling us.

HOWARD THOMAS: Ypres, Hill 62, Mount Sorrel.

HALF-BLOOD: MacGuinty uses me for my "Indian skills."

MACGUINTY: I need you out in no man's land, Woodrow. Slow and quiet, like I know you can.

BAM-BAM: Germany marches forward. The French cannot hold him back.

HALF-BLOOD: Night. Under the shadow of the moon. I hunt.

HALF-BLOOD gets into a trench with a German soldier.

HALF-BLOOD tries to slit the German's throat. It is not clean. The soldier thrashes and flails about madly.

Flares burst in the sky.

BAM-BAM: Freeze. When the flare goes up.

DICKEY: That's when machine gunners look for movement.

HALF-BLOOD: The fighting happens in the dark. Trench raids. Surging rivers. Tripwires, razor pits, murder holes.

BAM-BAM: Digging, digging, digging, it's all we do!

MACGUINTY: Clam it, Bam-Bam!

HALF-BLOOD: I start marking my kills on the hilt of my shovel—four.

HALF-BLOOD comes across German soldiers sleeping in the trenches. He clubs them to death with the shovel.

MACGUINTY: How you holding up, Doc?

HOWARD THOMAS: Limbs blown to hell. Trench rot. Chemical burns . . . it's a lot, Sarn't.

HALF-BLOOD: Seven, eight, nine, ten . . .

DICKEY: Dear Winnifred, when I get back home I've decided that I'm going to make you my wife.

BAM-BAM: Look here, boys, tie the piece of *fromage* to the end of your rifle, and when the rats get curious . . . Bam! Bam!

MACGUINTY: I need you back out there tonight, son.

The drumbeat picks up.

HALF-BLOOD: Sun and moon circle round and round. Fall covers no man's land in pounding rain. The corpses freeze at night when the cold winds come.

HALF-BLOOD sneaks into a mortar pit with a German sentry.

He uses his trench knives to stab the German behind the ears, up into the skull. This kill is better. Cleaner.

BAM-BAM: Hey, Doc, can you take a look at this?

HOWARD THOMAS: Trench foot.

BAM-BAM: Mais non.

HOWARD THOMAS: *Mais* yes. Take care of that, Bam-Bam, or it's coming off.

HALF-BLOOD: Thirteen, fourteen, fifteen, sixteen . . .

DICKEY: Did you see that Jerry-smasher that he made?

HOWARD THOMAS: Command asked us not to alter our kits like that.

BAM-BAM: Who cares, Doc? Fritz is scared of him.

DICKEY: *I'm* scared of him.

HALF-BLOOD: This war keeps getting worse. Each battle is more bloody.

MACGUINTY passes military patches down the line.

MACGUINTY: All right, lads. The Brits can't tell us Canadians apart from the other colonials. This red patch will identify you as a Canadian infantry soldier.

The soldiers attach red patches to both shoulders.

BAM-BAM: Finalement. I'm sick of being confuse with those guys de Newfoundland.

DICKEY: And they're sick of being confused with you, Frenchie.

MACGUINTY: Here you go, Woodrow. A red patch for a red man.

The men are in the trenches.

HALF-BLOOD: Spring rain fills the crater holes. All the water goes bad with the rotting flesh.

HOWARD THOMAS: Take your match and run the flame through the seams of your jacket. That way you can burn away all the lice.

BAM-BAM: Lice! Rats! My feet always wet. It's driving me crazy!

DICKEY: The new recruits they send us are goddamn useless.

BAM-BAM: All they do is stand up and get shot.

HOWARD THOMAS: Boys, it's our job to keep it together.

MACGUINTY: Woodrow. Trenches. Again.

Drums. Louder.

HALF-BLOOD: Twenty-one, twenty-two, twenty-three, twenty-four . . .

BAM-BAM: Doc, my foot is killing me!

HOWARD THOMAS: You got to keep your foot dry, Bam-Bam.

BAM-BAM: How am I supposed to do that?

DICKEY: Did MacGuinty send Woodrow back out there tonight?

HOWARD THOMAS: No.

BAM-BAM: He just keeps going back out.

Drums. Faster.

HOWARD THOMAS: Easy on the rum rations, Bam-Bam. MacGuinty will string you up if he finds you with that.

BAM-BAM: *Ostie*, Doc, the sarn't ain't going to say shit!

MACGUINTY: I've lost most of my unit, and you want me to order more of the boys to go over the top!?

HALF-BLOOD: Thirty-two, thirty-three, thirty-four, thirty-five . . .

HOWARD THOMAS: He's worrying me.

DICKEY: Who?

HALF-BLOOD: Thirty-seven, thirty-eight, thirty-nine, forty . . .

BAM-BAM: Saw him coming out of no man's land this morning. He was cover in blood.

HOWARD THOMAS: Should we say something to the sarn't?

BAM-BAM: "Sergeant, he's killing Germans, and he's great at it!"

HALF-BLOOD: Forty-three, forty-four, forty-five, forty-six . . .

The drums near their peak.

HOWARD THOMAS: Hey, Sarn't . . .

MACGUINTY: Doc.

DICKEY: Dear Winny. This place is weighing on us.

BAM-BAM: Notre père qui es aux cieux. *[Our God in Heaven.]*

HALF-BLOOD: Forty-nine, fifty, fifty-one, fifty-two . . .

HOWARD THOMAS: I'd like to recommend Woodrow for rest leave.

MACGUINTY: Rest leave?

HOWARD THOMAS: Yes.

DICKEY: It's like being in Hell.

HALF-BLOOD: Fifty-six, fifty-seven, fifty-eight, fifty-nine . . .

BAM-BAM: Délivre nous du mal. *[Deliver us from evil.]*

MACGUINTY: *Everyone* could use rest leave.

DICKEY: Please, Winny, write me back.

HALF-BLOOD: One night I come across a German in a machine gun pit.

HOWARD THOMAS: I know, but Seargeant Woodrow is—

BAM-BAM: S'il vous plaît, laissez nous partir d'ici. [*Please, let us leave this place.*]

HALF-BLOOD: I bring my shovel down so hard on his neck—

DICKEY: Winny?

BAM-BAM: Amen.

HALF-BLOOD: I hit his heart.

HOWARD THOMAS: Sarn't!

MACGUINTY / HALF-BLOOD: ENOUGH!

HALF-BLOOD strikes the German. The drums stop.

MACGUINTY: You want to go home? Win this bloody war and we'll all go home.

JONATHON appears next to HALF-BLOOD.

JONATHON: You were great!

HALF-BLOOD: Huh?

JONATHON: *You* were great out there.

HALF-BLOOD: What?

JONATHON: It's me.

HALF-BLOOD: Jonathon?

JONATHON: The brass sent me in.

HALF-BLOOD: But didn't you—?

JONATHON: I was fighting off in the 147th. My platoon got hacked down at the Somme, so they sent me over to you.

HALF-BLOOD: That's . . . this is incredible!

JONATHON: I missed you.

HALF-BLOOD: I *missed* you.

JONATHON: I've heard all about you in my unit. They're saying you're one of the greatest warriors we have.

HALF-BLOOD: They are?

JONATHON: You still got it?

HALF-BLOOD: What?

JONATHON: Your grandmother's medicine bag. It must be good luck.

HALF-BLOOD: I have it.

JONATHON: You and me. Real warriors. Just like we always said.

HALF-BLOOD: Warriors.

JONATHON: Take my hand, Half-Blood.

JONATHON reaches out. HALF-BLOOD takes his hand.

Don't let go.

LEAH SIMONE BOWEN
THE FLOOD

Leah Simone Bowen is a Toronto-based writer, producer, and Dora Mavor Moore Award–nominated director. She is the creator and co-host, along with Falen Johnson, of the CBC podcast *The Secret Life of Canada* about the untold and under-told history of the country. She is a graduate of the University of Alberta's theatre program.

In 1887, women were property and could be imprisoned for any reason. Jail was considered a place for the criminal, the disabled, the mentally ill, and the marginalized. Inspired by true accounts and the history of Toronto's St. Lawrence Market, *The Flood* gives voice to the little-known stories of early female prisoners in Canada. Warning: this excerpt contains strong language.

The Flood was first performed at St. Lawrence Hall, Toronto, on March 6, 2016, and produced by Toronto's First Post Office.

* * *

The market is loud, lots of foot traffic, laughter, etc. The GUARD
arrives with a pail.

OFFSTAGE VOICE ONE: Potatoes and carrots!

OFFSTAGE VOICE TWO: Apples by the bite and the barrel!

GUARD: Food! Bowls up!

*The cell doors open and all of the women step out in line with
their food bowls. They are served a grey slop porridge.*

Eat!!!

They begin to eat.

OFFSTAGE VOICE ONE: Watch yer feet, boys!!!

A huge amount of slosh begins to fall from above.

SOPHIA: Jesus Christ!!! We're trying to eat down here!!

The OFFSTAGE VOICES *laugh, conversations continue from above,
more slop comes down.*

The women in the prison start to object.

Every day with this. You bloody assholes!! I can see you, you— I know
you can see us!!!

More slosh lands straight into IRISH MARY'S *bowl. She drops it and
almost throws up. Fed up, she stands on a crate.*

IRISH MARY: There are women down here!

We hear the women of the prison agree.

SOPHIA: If I was up there I'd knife all of y'all. Did you hear me? You're dead . . .

IRISH MARY starts to sing to the tune of "Roll the Old Chariot" (traditional) to the market above.

IRISH MARY: Oh we'd be all right if we could eat a meal in peace!

She encourages the women to join her. We hear many voices, not just the onstage ones.

ALL: We'd be all right
If we could eat a meal in peace!
We'd be all right
If we could eat a meal in peace!
And we'll all hang on behind

And we'll roll the old chariot along,
We'll roll the old chariot along

We'll roll the old chariot along
And we'll all hang on behind

IRISH MARY: And no more iron bars
Wouldn't do us any harm!

ALL: And no more iron bars
Wouldn't do us any harm, and no more

Iron bars wouldn't do us any harm,
And we'll all hang on behind

And we'll roll the old chariot along,
We'll roll the old chariot along

We'll roll the old chariot along
And we'll all hang on behind

IRISH MARY: And walkin' overhead won't make us go away!

ALL: Oh walkin' overhead won't make us go away
Oh walkin' overhead won't make us go away
And we'll all hang on behind!

> *Cheers from the women and silence from above. Everyone goes back to eating.*

MARY: That was good; they've never stopped before.

IRISH MARY: They do it on purpose, don't they? It's disgusting, we're still people.

MARY: Here, take mine.

> *MARY offers her food to IRISH MARY.*

IRISH MARY: No, 'sides, it tastes terrible.

MARY: I'm convinced it's old glue, but eat.

IRISH MARY: I can't eat yours.

MARY: You must—we will share then. You need it for the baby.

IRISH MARY: The baby thinks it tastes terrible too.

SOPHIA pulls a cigarette out of her pocket and lights it.

SOPHIA: So, the new girl stops the slosh pouring over our heads.

IRISH MARY: We all did.

SOPHIA: It was fucking brave.

IRISH MARY: I don't think it was bravery exactly, but it didn't seem right what they were doing.

SOPHIA: Oh you're a Shant. I thought they would have another jail for the Irish.

IRISH MARY: What are you sayin'? You're a Darkie!

SOPHIA: A Darkie who was born in these parts, which you ain't, Shant.

IRISH MARY: I didn't grow up in a shanty, and I was working in a nice, respectable house here.

SOPHIA: And you brought shame on the house. When's the whoreson gonna be born?

IRISH MARY: I ain't a whore and I'm not gonna discuss my private business with you, thanks.

SOPHIA: It doesn't look too private to me; it looks like it's arriving soon. Plus, there are no secrets. We're all great friends, aren't we?

MARY: (*to* IRISH MARY) Ignore her.

IRISH MARY begins to eat again but dry heaves.

Pretend it's fish stew.

SOPHIA: (*mocking* MARY) Pretend it's fish stew. Ya certainly smell like fish stew. Imagine, they let a potato-picker live down here with us. I certainly hope you're not diseased.

IRISH MARY: What are you sayin'? You're the one with scabs all over your face—you look like you've got the plague.

SOPHIA: You're a brave little thing, aren't you? Or stupid. I haven't really decided yet. Obviously the wagon-burner didn't explain to you how things work, so let me.

SOPHIA grabs IRISH MARY by the hair.

You don't stand on any fucking crates again to try and pretend you have a place here. Do you understand me, bitch?

This floor you're standing on, food your eating, everything around you is mine. I own it. You're in my part of the cells. I own that invalid, the old hag, the Indian, and now you.

They all know if you want to live well and be left alone you don't fucking talk back. Are you listening? Irish whore, tell me you understand?

IRISH MARY nods her head.

SOPHIA shakes her.

Speak.

IRISH MARY: Yes!

MARY: Let her go.

SOPHIA: Oh wonderful, now I have two disobedient bitches on my hands.

MARY: She's pregnant.

SOPHIA: Ring the bells! A cat-lick twat got knocked up, what an event to be cherished.

MARY: I'm just saying leave her be; she don't know better.

SOPHIA: But you do and you're still flappin' you ugly mouth—it's all I can do to stand to look at you. Dirty Indian. I know your kind; I know your kind better than you do and I know not to trust you as far as I can spit.

SOPHIA spits in MARY's face to no reaction. She slaps MARY in the face and MARY slaps her back. SOPHIA gets MARY in a headlock.

IRISH MARY: Stop, please stop!

IRISH MARY grabs a piss bucket from the cell and throws it onto SOPHIA.

SOPHIA: You bitch. You harpie bitch!!!!

SOPHIA pulls out a knife.

I'm gonna fucking cut that baby out of you! Do you hear me? I'll fuckin' kill you!!!!!

The GUARD enters and pulls SOPHIA away.

GUARD: Hey!!! What's going on here?

IRISH MARY: I'm sorry, I poured the piss pot over her head.

GUARD: A knife, eh? That means it's the chains for you.

SOPHIA: What are you talkin'?

GUARD: There are no knives allowed down here.

SOPHIA: You gave me this!

GUARD: The rules are for everybody.

SOPHIA: Really!!? That's not what you told me last night, or the night before, or the night before that!!

He punches SOPHIA hard and then grabs her and chains her to the wall.

GUARD: (*to SOPHIA*) You don't know me.

SOPHIA: Please.

GUARD: Everyone back in 'er cell.

He exits.

IRISH MARY: I'm so sorry, Mary; I didn't know. I didn't know she was so crazy!

MARY: It's okay, I should have warned you

IRISH MARY: What's wrong with her?

MARY: I don't know, she's strange. Just don't get in her way. We're on her bad side now, but if we keep silent she'll forget about us soon. Thanks for helping me. I never had anyone stick up for me using a pail of piss before.

IRISH MARY: It was a terrible thing, wasn't it? I'll ask God for forgiveness.

MARY: It was the nicest thing anyone's ever done for me in a long time.

OUTWARD

MARJORIE CHAN
A NANKING WINTER

Marjorie is an award-winning writer born and raised in Toronto.
Her works have been performed in English and Cantonese in the US,
Scotland, Hong Kong, Russia, and across Canada. Her plays include
China Doll, *The Madness of the Square*, *a nanking winter*, *Tails From the
City*, as well as the libretti for the operas, *Sanctuary Song*, *The Lesson
of Da Ji*, *M'dea Undone*, and *The Monkiest King*. For her works, she has
been recognized with four Dora Mavor Moore Awards (for writing,
one for performance) a MyTheatre Award for Outstanding New Large
Work, a Harold Award, the K.M. Hunter Artist Award, and the George
Luscombe Award (for mentorship in professional theatre) as well as
nominations for the Governor General's Literary Award, Canadian
Citizen Award, and John Hirsch Prize for directing. Marjorie was the
artistic director of Cahoots Theatre from 2013 to 2019 and is currently Artistic Director of Theatre Passe Muraille.

Irene Wu has dedicated years of her life to researching the invasion
of Nanking, China. Through the winter of 1937, the Japanese Imperial
Army led a horrific campaign through the streets of China's capital,
an event that has been left unknown and untold to the world. Irene
is on the brink of releasing her research when her publisher voices
doubts about the book.

a nanking winter was first performed at Factory Theatre, Toronto, on
February 27, 2008, and was produced by Nightwood Theatre in association with Cahoots Theatre.

* * *

AUDREY: Where are the books? Are they in your car?

JULIA: Oh no no no, the company's sending them here. No worries, no worries. I saw the finished cover; they look great. They'll look fantastic! And I know they finally shipped out to stores yesterday. Kurt explained? It was just a delay.

IRENE: What exactly happened?

JULIA: Does it even matter? Look, I don't want you to worry your little head. A little controversy never hurt a new writer.

FRANK: Especially one writing *non-fiction*!

JULIA: The books'll be here soon enough.

FRANK: Good. Gotta pick up my kid by eight. My week with him. His mother goes bitch-crazy when I don't pick him up on time.

JULIA: Frank . . . please.

FRANK: *(continuing)* I mean, she works from home, what difference does it make?

JULIA: So! Have you two packed and got your things sorted?

A beat.

IRENE: Excuse me?

JULIA: For the book tour?

IRENE: Oh. Kurt's not coming on the tour.

JULIA: He's not?

KURT: Actually, my parents'll probably retire in Japan so I'm back at the restaurant full-time.

JULIA: Okay.

JULIA and FRANK look at each other.

JULIA: It's just you do realize, it's quite a long tour; you're lucky to get it. Fourteen dates across North America, starting here and moving east . . .

IRENE: And you'll be coming?

JULIA: Of course! Not in every city. But, definitely. Definitely. I'll definitely try. It's only—well—are you comfortable travelling all by yourself?

IRENE: I don't need a babysitter.

JULIA: I wasn't suggesting you did! I thought you might want a companion. Maybe Audrey? Hartford's pulling out all the stops, first-class hotels, first-class airfare. Lots of time for sightseeing.

AUDREY: Wow.

JULIA: Audrey, what do you say? You never know, we may even get over the pond! Hartford's still working out the details, but translations are on the way. Strong interest, very strong interest. German, definitely, obviously. French. Danish interest for some reason! UK version, but I told you that already . . .

IRENE: Mandarin? Cantonese?

JULIA: Well . . .

IRENE: Korean?

JULIA: Irene—

IRENE: Japanese?

JULIA: No.

IRENE: No Asian translations?

JULIA: Listen, we do a North American run, and, and Europe looks pretty good, promising. And . . . it's a delay in Asia, that's all. After they see the sales, they won't need convincing. We don't want to release the book without the proper research into the market. We research, we wait, and the book is released in the proper climate. You don't want your book to be a bust, do you? And we certainly don't want a repeat of your last time in Japan.

KURT: No, I agree.

JULIA: You are not a complete unknown in these circles. They have been misquoting your articles for years!

IRENE: I was a business reporter.

JULIA: Who occasionally strayed into cultural territory in her pieces. Which brought you to my attention.

IRENE: So it's my fault?

JULIA: So we want to be careful how we proceed.

FRANK: Very careful.

JULIA eyes FRANK.

JULIA: Hartford's going to be very happy. And very happy to have you along . . . Audrey?

AUDREY: Okay! It's not like I'm doing anything else!

JULIA: Okay!

IRENE: So, I guess I don't have a say!

JULIA: Irene— It'll be lovely. A lovely tour. You know, the publishers are really behind you. They believe in you and what you're trying to say. They're gonna promote the hell outta this book, don't you worry. Hartford & Ross wants everyone who's anyone to have your name on their lips. We want every major paper to review your book. We want it taught in universities. We want you booked into every talk show, every discussion panel. We want you to be the go-to Chinese writer.

IRENE: For what? For everything?

JULIA: No, no. Of course not. Not everything. Relevant things, naturally. Political things, women's issues, you know, Darfur or even the Bosnian women, Pakistan . . .

IRENE: I'm not a specialist in any of those areas . . .

JULIA: Well, you don't have to be a specialist to be on a panel! That's the whole point. They start the conversation about genocide or some such thing and, from there, you cite an example from your book and talk about Nanking blah blah blah. Get it? Now, you've mentioned your book—and someone somewhere out there in TV land—someone will go out and buy it!

IRENE: Okay.

FRANK: Well, no, you can't just go out there and say anything!

JULIA: No, of course, no no no. That's not what I meant. No, you most definitely can't—

FRANK: So tomorrow, we'll meet early, with my team, and we'll go over a few things. Lines of argument, phrasing, that kind of thing.

IRENE: What?

FRANK: If you're really concerned, we can email you our notes. I mean, it's all your material, we've just organized quotations—direct from your book, mind you—we've organized them into arguments. We do it for all our non-fiction writers. Sometimes we have to do it for our fiction writers too, don't we?

IRENE: I don't understand, Frank. Who, who are you?

FRANK: Didn't she tell you? Didn't she tell you why I'm here?

JULIA: I haven't had the chance . . .

FRANK: Frank Sadowitch, Hartford & Ross & Company. Legal Department.

IRENE: Oh.

FRANK: You do understand, right, that a book that is as controversial as yours—there are things that raise a few eyebrows. For starters, your accusations toward the current Japanese government and the royal family!

IRENE: I was very thorough, Mr. Sadowitch. My references, my research—

FRANK: Yes, your research. Very impressive. We went through your book with a fine-toothed comb. I tell ya, I wasn't sure though. That first draft I read. I thought, a Nazi hero, what the fuck!

IRENE: Okay . . .

FRANK: Sorry. Never start talking about Nazis in polite company, it's bound to go badly.

JULIA: Frank—

FRANK: But I mean, he was a Nazi for godsakes!

IRENE: Niklas Herrmann was de-nazified just before he died. In fact, in his diaries, he says that—

FRANK: Discovering his diary! Now that—is priceless! Good thing his son let you have it!

IRENE: He didn't initially. Until he trusted me. I had to go back day after day.

FRANK: I mean the amount of research that you recovered— The diary, the secret photos, the letters to Hitler! What a great story. It'd make a great movie.

JULIA: Oh yeah! A movie!

FRANK: You could call it *Nazi of Nanking*!

JULIA: Or maybe *Niklas of Nanking* . . .

FRANK: And then that American woman . . . What was her name? The missionary . . . the sister who taught at the college . . . Gin-a-ling.

IRENE: Ginling College. Her name was Anna Mallery.

FRANK: Anna Mallery—is that not a name for a movie character or what? And talk about tragic! Her life was tragic! Now that's an ending! You could call that movie *Nun of Nanking*! Make a whole series!

JULIA: Frank . . .

FRANK: *Nicky and the Nun*!

IRENE: (*a correction*) Anna Mallery and Niklas Herrmann are both considered heroes in China. They were at the centre of the entire safety zone operation, saving thousands of lives.

FRANK: I'm just happy you decided to beef up those sections. It made a huge shift for me, in terms of the growth of your book. A huge shift. I mean, without it . . . I don't know too much about Sino-Japanese relations and all. It's a big blur. But you get the foreign nationals in—gives me a focus for the story—

IRENE: It's not a "story." It's not fiction.

JULIA: You know what he means—a narrative approach to non-fiction . . . shaping the information in a way that engages your audience. You have to know your audience! Academics, historians, and Chinese advocates, yes, fine, a very small market. But including the Western witnesses gives your book better range and broader appeal!

IRENE: What?!

JULIA: You want to tell this story, right? Well, when you're able to tell it from a Western point of view—this is the English reader after all, this is where the market is—

IRENE: Wait. Wait. Let me just get this straight. You're saying that it's good that I included the foreigners because *it will sell more books*!?!

JULIA: No, not just that. That wasn't what I was saying at all!

IRENE: So what are you saying?

FRANK: Telling the truth is a good thing. Telling the truth about the Americans and Germans, yes even Nazis who were able to save the Chinese people—

IRENE: They saved *some* Chinese people. They didn't save *the* Chinese people.

FRANK: You didn't let me finish. The Chinese people of Nanking. The Westerners set up the safety zone, didn't they? That's what your research says?

IRENE: Yes, of course . . .

FRANK: At great risk to their own lives?

IRENE: Right—but—

FRANK: And what was the Chinese army doing? What were the officials of Nanking doing?

IRENE: They were being invaded!

FRANK: And weren't they also in retreat from the city? Leaving it virtually defenseless? In your book, you said that the Chinese army was ill-equipped and unprepared. That they were ineffective! Didn't you write that? I didn't write that.

IRENE: But the Chinese didn't have the power! Niklas Herrmann had influence because of the colour of his skin, the swastika on his sleeve. That meant something to the Japanese.

FRANK: I think we're saying the same thing, aren't we?

IRENE: No, I don't think we are! You're saying that representing these Western heroes with prominence is a way to make it more palatable for a Western audience.

JULIA: Irene—now don't get—

IRENE: That it's more convenient to paint the Chinese as helpless against the ruthless Japanese, so helpless and useless that a group of foreign nationals, and by foreign, I think that you mean white, that these foreigners have to rescue them?

FRANK: That's not the slant I was going for—

IRENE: Bad Japs rape and kill dumb Chinks. Good white people save the day. Is that more the *slant* you were going for?

FRANK: Now come on!

AUDREY: Irene!

FRANK: I don't have to put up with this! You can't say that!

IRENE: You're not going to tell me what I can and cannot say!

JULIA: Irene. That's his job!

KURT: Just calm down—

IRENE: I don't care if it's his job! He's in my living room, throwing around his elitist, racist comments—

FRANK: What is your problem here, really? Because I'll tell you what I think it is. It's not that you think the "foreigners," the "white people" didn't save those people in Nanking. It's because deep down you know they did. All your extensive research backs that up. And what gets you, what really gets you, is that you wish it weren't true. You wish that the Chinese could've been more organized, fought back, done anything! But they didn't. They couldn't. They lay down and they were slaughtered! It was their own fault!

IRENE: What!?!!!!!

KURT: THAT'S ENOUGH! ENOUGH! LET'S JUST DO THIS!!

IRENE: *Do what?*

JULIA: We have to tell you something.

KURT: I think you should sit down.

IRENE: Is there a problem?

JULIA: Well, we wanted to talk to you about the title.

IRENE: We've been over this.

JULIA: You know, compromise is a part of life. When we last were able to communicate—while you were away—we discussed the final title change.

IRENE: No, of course it's changed. The title is *Nanking—The Other Holocaust*.

FRANK: This is what we wanted to talk to you about.

IRENE: They let my original title stand? It *is The Nanking Holocaust*?

FRANK: Absolutely not.

IRENE: I'm sorry, I'm confused. My original title, *The Nanking Holocaust*, wasn't approved, right?

JULIA: Yes. There were many objections, as you know.

IRENE: I know. They didn't like the word "holocaust."

JULIA: A word with too many connotations. They felt you could *appear* to be *trying* to draw on sympathy—

IRENE: I'm not trying to take anything away from anyone.

JULIA: I know. But a *perception* that you were—

IRENE: I was using a word. In the proper context. If it wasn't in a title it would be "holocaust" with a small "h." Holocaust: from the Greek. *Holos*, meaning whole. *Kaustos*, meaning burned. Completely burned.

JULIA: It's too evocative and it was always unlikely to pass . . .

IRENE: But the compromise? What we decided on—

JULIA: I thought they might go for it, but y'know I had some questions myself—

IRENE: *Nanking—The Other Holocaust.* What's wrong with that?

FRANK: They liked that one even less.

IRENE: Why? That doesn't make any sense!

FRANK: The issue was primarily the "other." Its implications were that Nanking was the other—

IRENE: That's what I wanted to imply!

JULIA: But by doing so, by implying that Nanking was the "other holocaust," by default you're also implying that the Holocaust was the only other one in history.

FRANK: Definitely more problematic than the first.

IRENE: So— What are you saying? What are you saying? That my book has gone to print with an unknown title!

JULIA: It was going to print. And you were in the hospital. Kurt and I couldn't find Audrey . . .

IRENE: What is the title?

JULIA: I consulted with legal and with Kurt. He had your power of attorney. We made a decision.

IRENE: What is the title, Julia?

JULIA: We made a decision that got your book on the shelves. We made a decision that would make sure people will read about Nanking!

IRENE: What is it!!

Beat.

JULIA: It's called *The Nanking Incident.*

Bigger beat.

KURT: Irene . . .

AUDREY: Omigod.

IRENE: I don't know what to say. I don't. Frankly—I'm shocked. I'm shocked and hurt that you, all of you, would let this happen.

JULIA: No, wait—

IRENE: *The Nanking Incident?* It wasn't an *incident.* It was far far worse and more horrible than an incident.

JULIA: I know, but let me explain our reasoning—

IRENE: There is no reasoning. There can't be any reason behind a decision like that! That title is absurd! It's ridiculous! It's not only reductive, it's revisionist!

JULIA: I want to talk about the revisionists! The people who've been harassing you, they were behind the delay . . .

IRENE: I gathered that.

JULIA: But this is precisely why we chose "incident."

IRENE: Because you're playing right into their hands. You're helping them to erase history. You're aiding a denial of war crimes on a massive scale. Diminishing any culpability, any responsibility—

JULIA: No, no, no, no—

IRENE: Then what? Yes! Please explain to me!

JULIA: If I was some kind of right-wing nut—which you know very well that I'm not—but if I was, and hell bent on Japanese nationalism, it would be much easier for me to argue against a Nanking *Holocaust* than a Nanking *Incident*. Do you see? There is too much evidence to deny an "*incident*." It would make those radicals seem completely irrational if they tried to do that. These groups would lose any credibility they had with moderate thinkers. Do you see? Do you see how it's a better choice?

IRENE: It's easier to build a case against a holocaust—

JULIA: Yes . . .

IRENE: But harder to build against an incident?

JULIA: Not harder—virtually impossible.

AUDREY: So the title . . . makes it more difficult for people to deny what happened.

JULIA: Exactly.

AUDREY: I see.

IRENE: I don't.

JULIA: I'm trying to help you, your book.

IRENE: Changing the title doesn't have to do with sales?

JULIA: Oh I would never presume to say that. Never. Doesn't selling more books help you?

IRENE: Yes—but . . .

JULIA: Say you're browsing in a big book store on a Saturday afternoon? You come across a series of books, each with the title *Holocaust* and *Massacre* and *Atrocity* and lastly *Incident*. Which one of those would you pick up?

WAJDI MOUAWAD, TRANSLATED BY LINDA GABORIAU
SCORCHED / INCENDIES

Wajdi Mouawad's plays have been translated into more than twenty languages and presented all over the world. In all his work, from his own plays and adaptations, from the productions he has directed to the novels he's written, Mouawad expresses the conviction that "art bears witness to human existence through the prism of beauty." He is the recipient of numerous awards and honours for his work and is currently Director of La Colline—théâtre national in Paris.

Linda Gaboriau is a literary translator and dramaturg based in Montreal. She has translated more than 120 plays. Her translations have been published and widely produced across Canada and abroad. Her work has garnered many awards, including the Governor General's Literary Award for Translation in 1996, and in 2010 for *Forests* and 2019 for *Birds of a Kind*, both by Wajdi Mouawad.

A mother falls into complete silence. Upon her death, her twin children are asked to uncover the source of that silence. They must find the father they never knew, and the brother they never knew they had. Their journey begins in Montreal but the answers lie in the rubble of a war-torn desert.

Scorched was first performed in English at the Tarragon Theatre, Toronto, on February 20, 2007, in a production by the Tarragon Theatre and the National Arts Centre, and was directed by Richard Rose.

Incendies was first presented in France, on March 14, 2003, at l'Hexagone Scène Nationale de Meylan, and subsequently in Québec, on May 23, 2003, at Théâtre de Quat'sous during the tenth edition of the Festival de théâtre des Amériques.

* * *

NAWAL *(age nineteen) and* SAWDA *in the orphanage in Kfar Rayat with a doctor.*

NAWAL: There was no one in the orphanage in Nabatiyé. We came here. To Kfar Rayat.

THE DOCTOR: You shouldn't have. There are no children here either.

NAWAL: Why?

THE DOCTOR: Because of the war.

SAWDA: What war?

THE DOCTOR: Who knows . . . Brothers are shooting their brothers and fathers are shooting their fathers. A war. But what war? One day 500,000 refugees arrived from the other side of the border and said: "They've chased us off our land, let us live side by side." Some people from here said yes, some people from here said no, some people from here fled. Millions of destinies. And no one knows who is shooting whom or why. It's a war.

NAWAL: And where are the children who were here?

THE DOCTOR: Everything happened so fast. The refugees arrived. They took all the children away. Even the newborn babies. Everyone. They were angry.

SAWDA: Why did the refugees take the children?

THE DOCTOR: Out of revenge. Two days ago, the militia hanged three young refugees who strayed outside the camps. Why did the militia hang the three teenagers? Because two refugees from the camp had raped and killed a girl from the village of Kfar Samira. Why did they rape the girl? Because the militia had stoned a family of refugees. Why did the militia stone them? Because the refugees had set fire to a house near the hill where thyme grows. Why did the refugees set fire to the house? To take revenge on the militia who had destroyed a well they had drilled. Why did the militia destroy the well? Because the refugees had burned the crop near the river where the dogs run. Why did they burn the crop? There must be a reason, that's as far as my memory goes, I can't retrace it any further, but the story can go on forever, one thing leading to another, from anger to anger, from sadness to grief, from rape to murder, back to the beginning of time.

NAWAL: Which way did they go?

THE DOCTOR: They were headed south. To the camps. Now everyone is afraid. We're expecting retaliation.

NAWAL: Did you know the children?

THE DOCTOR: I was their doctor.

NAWAL: I'm trying to find a child.

THE DOCTOR: You'll never find him.

NAWAL: I will find him. A boy of four. He arrived here a few days after his birth. Old Elhame delivered him from my belly and took him away.

THE DOCTOR: And why did you give him to her?

NAWAL: They took him away from me! I didn't give him away! They took him from me. Was he here?

THE DOCTOR: Elhame brought many children.

NAWAL: Yes, but she didn't bring many in the spring four years ago. A newborn boy. From the North. Do you have records?

THE DOCTOR: No more records.

NAWAL: A cleaning woman, a kitchen worker, someone who would remember. Remember having found the child beautiful. Having taken him from Elhame.

THE DOCTOR: I'm a doctor, not an administrator. I travel around to all the orphanages. I can't know everything. Go look in the camps, down south.

NAWAL: Where did the children sleep?

THE DOCTOR: In this ward.

NAWAL: Where are you? Where are you?

JANINE: Mama, what are you looking at?

NAWAL: Now that we're together, everything feels better.

JANINE: What did you mean by that?

NAWAL: Now that we're together, everything feels better.

JANINE: Now that we're together, everything feels better.

Night. Hospital. ANTOINE comes running in.

ANTOINE: What? What? Nawal? Nawal!

SAWDA: Nawal!

ANTOINE: What did you say? Nawal!

ANTOINE picks a tape recorder up off the floor beside NAWAL (age sixty-four).

NAWAL: If I could turn back the clock, he would still be in my arms . . .

SAWDA: Where are you going? Where are you going?

ANTOINE picks up the phone and dials a number.

ANTOINE: Janine Marwan . . . ?

NAWAL: South.

ANTOINE: Antoine Ducharme, your mother's nurse.

SAWDA: Wait! Nawal! Wait!

ANTOINE: She just spoke. Nawal just spoke.

NAWAL exits.

* * *

NAWAL (19 ans) et SAWDA dans l'orphelinat de Kfar Rayat.

NAWAL: À l'orphelinat de Nabatiyé il n'y avait personne. On est venues ici. À Kfar Rayat.

LE MÉDECIN: Vous n'auriez pas dû. Ici non plus il n'y a plus d'enfants.

NAWAL: Pourquoi?

LE MÉDECIN: C'est la guerre.

SAWDA: Quelle guerre?

LE MÉDECIN: Qui sait? Personne ne comprend. Les frères tirent sur leurs frères et les pères sur leurs pères. Une guerre. Mais quelle guerre? Un jour 500 000 réfugiés sont arrivés de l'autre côté de la frontière. Ils ont dit: « On nous a chassés de nos terres, laissez-nous vivre à vos côtés. » Des gens d'ici ont dit oui, des gens d'ici ont dit non, des gens d'ici ont fui. Des millions de destins. Et on ne sait plus qui tire sur qui ni pourquoi. C'est la guerre.

NAWAL: Et les enfants qui étaient ici, où sont-ils?

LE MÉDECIN: Tout s'est passé très vite. Les réfugiés sont arrivés. Ils ont pris tout le monde. Même les nouveau-nés. Tout le monde. Ils étaient en colère.

SCORCHED / INCENDIES | 69

LE MÉDECIN: Pour se venger. Il y a deux jours, les miliciens ont pendu trois adolescents réfugiés qui se sont aventurés en dehors des camps. Pourquoi les miliciens ont-ils pendu les trois adolescents? Parce que deux réfugiés du camp avaient violé et tué une fille du village de Kfar Samira. Pourquoi ces deux types ont-ils violé cette fille? Parce que les miliciens avaient lapidé une famille de réfugiés. Pourquoi les miliciens l'ont-ils lapidée? Parce que les réfugiés avaient brûlé une maison près de la colline du thym. Pourquoi les réfugiés ont-ils brûlé la maison? Pour se venger des miliciens qui avaient détruit un puits d'eau foré par eux. Pourquoi les miliciens ont détruit le puits? Parce que des réfugiés avaient brûlé une récolte du côté du fleuve au chien. Pourquoi ont-ils brûlé la récolte? Il y a certainement une raison, ma mémoire s'arrête là, je ne peux pas monter plus haut, mais l'histoire peut se poursuivre encore longtemps, de fil en aiguille, de colère en colère, de peine en tristesse, de viol en meurtre, jusqu'au début du monde.

NAWAL: Ils sont partis où?

LE MÉDECIN: Vers le sud. Dans les camps. Maintenant tout le monde a peur. On attend les représailles.

NAWAL: Vous connaissiez les enfants?

LE MÉDECIN: Je suis le médecin qui les soignait.

NAWAL: Je veux retrouver un enfant.

LE MÉDECIN: Vous ne le retrouverez plus.

NAWAL: Je le trouverai. Un enfant de quatre ans. Il est arrivé ici quelques jours après sa naissance. C'est la vieille Elhame qui l'a sorti de mon ventre et l'a emporté.

LE MÉDECIN: Et vous, pourquoi l'avez-vous donné?

NAWAL: On me l'a pris! Je ne l'ai pas donné. On me l'a pris! Est-ce qu'il était ici?

LE MÉDECIN: Elhame apportait beaucoup d'enfants à Kfar Rayat.

NAWAL: Oui, mais elle n'en a pas apporté beaucoup vers le printemps d'il y a quatre ans. Un nouveau-né. Un garçon. Venu du Nord. Vous avez un registre?

LE MÉDECIN: Plus de registre.

NAWAL: Une femme de ménage, une cantinière, quelqu'un qui se souvient. Se souvient d'avoir trouvé l'enfant beau. De l'avoir pris des mains d'Elhame.

LE MÉDECIN: Je suis médecin, pas administrateur. Je fais le tour de tous les orphelinats. Je ne peux pas tout savoir. Allez voir dans les camps. Au sud.

NAWAL: Et les enfants, où dormaient-ils?

LE MÉDECIN: Dans cette salle.

NAWAL: Où es-tu? Où es-tu?

JEANNE: Qu'est-ce que tu regardes, maman?

NAWAL: Maintenant que nous sommes ensemble, ça va mieux.

JEANNE: Qu'est-ce que tu as voulu dire par là?

NAWAL: Maintenant que nous sommes ensemble, ça va mieux.

JEANNE: Maintenant que nous sommes ensemble, ça va mieux.

Nuit. Hôpital. ANTOINE arrive en courant.

ANTOINE: Quoi? Quoi?? Nawal! Nawal!

SAWDA: Nawal!

ANTOINE: Qu'est-ce que vous avez dit? Nawal!

ANTOINE ramasse un enregistreur aux pieds de NAWAL (64 ans).

NAWAL: Si je pouvais reculer le temps, il serait dans mes bras . . .

SAWDA: Où vas-tu?

ANTOINE: Mademoiselle Jeanne Marwan?

NAWAL: Au sud.

ANTOINE: Antoine Ducharme, infirmier de votre mère.

SAWDA: Attends! Attends! Nawal, attends!

ANTOINE: Elle a parlé, votre mère a parlé.

NAWAL sort.

ANOSH IRANI
THE MEN IN WHITE

Anosh Irani has published four critically acclaimed novels: *The Cripple and His Talismans*, *The Song of Kahunsha*, *Dahanu Road*, and *The Parcel*. His play *Bombay Black* won five Dora Mavor Moore Awards, including for Outstanding New Play, and his anthology *The Bombay Plays* was shortlisted for the Governor General's Literary Award, as was *The Men in White*. His latest play, *Buffoon*, won the 2020 Dora Mavor Moore Award for Outstanding New Play. His work has been translated into eleven languages.

Eighteen-year-old Hasan Siddiqui escapes the drudgery of his work at a slaughterhouse by fostering two fervent dreams—to become a star in cricket and to win the affections of Haseena, a fiercely intelligent young woman two years his junior. Half a world away in Vancouver, Hasan's older brother, Abdul, has been working under the table at an Indian restaurant, attempting to set down roots with the hope of one day reuniting with his brother. For Abdul the immigrant dream shows little sign of materializing, but he finds solace in his amateur cricket team. When he and the team's captain decide to take action to end their losing streak, they talk of recruiting the talented Hasan for the rest of the season. But bringing Hasan from India to Canada will take much more than just a plane ticket, and rising tensions demonstrate that not all members of the team agree with the high cost.

The Men in White was first produced at the Arts Club Theatre Company's Granville Island Stage, Vancouver, on February 15, 2017, and received its Toronto premiere at the Factory Theatre on October 18, 2018.

* * *

The locker room.

Everyone is dressed in whites.

SAM and ABDUL are in the room.

SAM is in full cricket gear, ready for the game. He is pacing about with his bat in hand. The game hasn't started yet.

ABDUL is seated on the bench. He is watching SAM.

ABDUL: Why you nervous?

SAM: It's the first game of the season. I hate first games.

ABDUL: You should not hate any game. Love all game. First game, last game, all same. All chance to play.

SAM: That's easy for you to say. You always score runs. And you're not even opening with me this time. That makes it worse.

ABDUL: Sam, why you play cricket?

SAM: What do you mean?

ABDUL: You Chinese. Why cricket? Chinese no cricketers.

SAM: As a kid, I was never good at sports. So I didn't have any friends. Except Ram. He moved from India and I moved from China at the same time. He's been my friend since the fifth grade. He let me play cricket with him. It made me feel . . . a part of something. And I saw just how much he loved the game. So it made me want to play even more.

ABDUL: Exactly. You saw him love. You saw him love game. What you doing, this not love. This fear.

SAM: But I am scared, do you mind?

ABDUL: What you scared of? Of scoring duck?

SAM: Let's not talk about ducks. I refuse to get out on zero in the first game.

ABDUL: But you will. Because you playing for wrong reason. You don't play because you scared of scoring zero. You play because want to make hundred.

SAM: I've never made a hundred. I never will.

A small pause. ABDUL wants to say something, but he is not sure. Then he goes for it.

ABDUL: You know Dongri in Bombay? Dongri area?

SAM: I've heard of it. Ram talks about it sometimes. I know what it's famous for.

ABDUL: For what?

SAM: Dawood Ibrahim.

ABDUL: Correct. Dawood Bhai. Dawood Bhai in Pakistan now. He stop coming India after bomb blasts in '93. Did you know Bhai policeman's son? Son of honest policeman? But Bhai become underworld don. Whole Dongri proud of Bhai. I hear stories of Bhai from older boys and I proud too. One day my baba ask me,

"What you proud of?" I say, "Baba, he become big man from small place like Dongri." Baba say, "Yes, Bhai become big man from small place. But you don't need to become big man. You need to become *good* man." When I little, Baba tell me parents die in bike accident. But now Baba tell hard truth. My father, he stuntman. One day, man from Dawood gang come to him. D-Company say we need you ride motorcycle. D-Company man sit behind you, you ride fast, D-Company kill, you ride faster. Father say no. For seven day, D-Company man come. Final warning. My father no killer. My father say no. One night D-Company man kill father. Mother also bullet. By mistake but. She next to father. I play cricket to forget. The longer I out there on pitch, less I think of Baba. Of Hasan. Of father, mother. So if I get out zero, I feel double worse than you. Then all week when I cook, I piss off. And then food taste pissy.

Beat.

You want to forget something? You score runs. Runs help forget.

SAM: No, man. I mean . . . sure, I have things . . . but nothing like yours.

ABDUL: Nothing you want forget?

SAM: I can't think of anything.

ABDUL: Thanks Allah for blessed life then.

SAM: Yeah, man.

ABDUL: But I give you secret.

SAM: Anything, man. Anything.

ABDUL: People make fun of you. They think you stupid . . . right?

SAM: Well . . . I mean . . . sometimes, but—

ABDUL: They think you stupid. *I* think you stupid.

SAM: Oh. Okay then. That's your secret?

ABDUL: Doc keep saying you not opening batsman. Randy feel bad for you so he take you in team. Treat you like disabled child case. You and Ram watch porno on phone all day. You no get chicks on own. You loser. Correct?

SAM: I'm beginning to get pissed off with you. And just so you know, *everyone* watches porn on their phones now. It's like checking the time. It just pops up, you know. You're trying to send a text to someone and suddenly you have these pink nipples in front of you, and your whole day goes for a toss and . . . why the hell am I explaining this to you? I'm pissed off with you.

ABDUL: Good, good. Now keep all piss, keep all it in your stomach, in heart, keep all piss off. On cricket field, all bowler your enemy. All bowler make fun of you. For watching porn, for spend Saturday night alone alone alone, for not good at anything, for never winning lottery.

SAM: The lottery?

ABDUL: You win lottery?

SAM: No. Never.

ABDUL: Then bowler fault.

SAM: Okay . . .

ABDUL: Use anger. Use insult. You walk out, you look bowler, and you insult! Don't matter who. India, Pakistan, Australia—

SAM: What about China?

ABDUL: China no play cricket. You problem China?

SAM: I'm in love with a Chinese girl. But her father won't let her see me.

ABDUL: Then China just announce entry into world cricket. Her father bowling at you. Her small China father coming for you. He want you dead. He want you choke on noodle. He want you have no tongue to kiss pretty daughter.

SAM: Actually, her father's a really nice guy. I think *she* doesn't like me.

ABDUL: Sam! Attention!

SAM: Sorry.

ABDUL: Forget China. Keep piss off anger.

ABDUL takes the bat from SAM.

So you walk down pitch with bat. You look bowler in eye. "I kill you. I burn your home. I kill your wife. I kill your child. I kill your child's child."

SAM: That's a lot of killing.

ABDUL: But you don't say! You just feel. You look in eyes and feel.

SAM: (*charged up*) Yes, I will burn your house. I will burn your brother. Your father. Your uncle. But I will save you and your wife. Then I will tie you up and make you watch while your wife and I . . . while your wife and I . . . watch porn together on my phone!

He slams his bat against his pads and strides out in a rage. He is SAM *the Batting Machine.*

As SAM *exits,* RANDY *enters.*

RANDY: What happened to him?

ABDUL: He just excited.

RANDY: That's good. I hate starting on a losing note.

DOC enters.

DOC: Sam's really pumped up. I hope he lasts out there.

ABDUL: Don't worry, he be out there long time.

RANDY: So Abdul. I discussed Hasan's situation with the boys again. There's two ways of getting him into the country. The first option is a bit complicated. The club has to bring him in an official capacity. So we write a letter saying we are importing Hasan Siddiqui to play for us for one season.

ABDUL: Oh, he be happy. If letter from club, dream come true. How you say here . . . "Awesome!"

RANDY: But for that we have to prove that a Canadian can't do what he does.

ABDUL: But Canadian cannot. Canadian good with ice. Canadian, how you say here . . . suck balls in cricket.

RANDY: But it's not like Hasan has a professional career in India. I mean, he's not playing for any club. So there's no proof of experience. And we'd have to advertise for one month, locally, in three different places to target the Canadian market. It's a pain in the ass.

Beat.

But there's a second way.

ABDUL: How?

RANDY: We bring him on a tourist visa. You write a letter saying that your brother would like to visit you for a couple of months. And then he plays.

ABDUL: He no visit me. I illegal here, man! Five years I hiding in back of restaurant. I report, *I* deport. I no write letter. I no even have *brother*.

RANDY: What do you mean?

ABDUL: Before coming Canada, I write in form. Zero family.

RANDY: Why'd you do that?

ABDUL: My sponsor say to do, so I do.

Beat.

Doc, you write letter for me? Please?

DOC: Well, it's not that simple.

ABDUL: Why? Simple. He come, he play, he go.

DOC: Right.

ABDUL: What you mean, Doc?

DOC: What do I mean about what?

ABDUL: "Right." What that mean?

DOC: For one, from what I've been told, your brother doesn't even have a bank account. The government wants to see that he has sufficient funds in his account.

ABDUL: I get funds. I do for Hasan.

DOC: How?

ABDUL: My problem. I figure.

DOC: Okay then.

ABDUL: So you give letter? You citizen. You doctor. Respected man. You give letter, Hasan get visa.

DOC: No, I no give letter.

RANDY: Hey, easy, Doc.

ABDUL: No, no, let him say what he feel. What you feel, Doc? Tell.

DOC doesn't respond. ABDUL is hurt but realizes he is in no position to start a confrontation.

But his hurt and shame don't subside.

(*to himself*) Why can't people just speak truth?

Now DOC latches on.

DOC: You want the truth? I'll give you the truth. I don't think your brother will go back, okay? I think he'll stay on, just like you. It's people like you who give Indians a bad name. You sneak into this country, you stay on, and you make it hard for people like us.

ABDUL: Like you? Like educated man? Man with money? So I no money, no study, so I thief?

DOC: You said it.

ABDUL is upset. His body language is a bit aggressive.

DOC senses this.

What—you want to hit me? That's all your people do. Blood is all you know.

ABDUL: My people?

RANDY: Doc, that's enough.

DOC tries to calm himself. But ABDUL continues.

ABDUL: So who my people, Doc? I Indian, you Indian. So who my people? How my people different from yours?

DOC: I'm Canadian.

ABDUL: Say it. You big man. You know names of diseases. But can't see own disease?

DOC: I'm not blind, Abdul. I can see. I have seen. I've seen what you did in Bombay. I saw what your people did during the riots!

ABDUL: Say it! Say the name!

RANDY: Guys, this is—

ABDUL: Say it!

DOC: You Muslims! Okay? I will not allow another Muslim to enter this country. This is my country now. Stay out of it!

DOC storms out.

RANDY: (*to ABDUL*) Don't worry about him. He's just . . .

Suddenly, RAM enters. He is supporting SAM, who is badly hurt.

SAM's face is bleeding. His white shirt is covered in blood.

RANDY immediately gets an ice pack and a towel.

What happened?

RAM: He got hit, that's what happened. I have no idea what got into him.

RANDY: What do you mean?

RAM: He played a couple of balls and then just started insulting the bowler. He told him to go watch porn. He said, "Your wife called. She said you forgot your balls at home."

RANDY: What the fuck?

RAM: The next ball the bowler gave him a bouncer straight on the nose.

RANDY: (*to SAM*) What the hell is wrong with you?

SAM: (*sounding nasal and in pain*) Ask him!

RANDY: Who?

SAM: Abdul! I was so charged up I forgot to wear my helmet!

RANDY: How much did you score?

SAM: A duck. Zero, man! Zero! A duck *and* a broken nose!

ABDUL picks up his bat and his cricket kit.

ABDUL: I win this game for you. I win this game. Abdul need to stay there long. Abdul need to forget.

He leaves.

CARMEN AGUIRRE
THE REFUGEE HOTEL

Carmen Aguirre is a Vancouver-based theatre artist who has worked extensively in North and South America. She has written and co-written twenty-one plays, including *Chile Con Carne*, *The Trigger*, *The Refugee Hotel*, and *Blue Box*. Her first non-fiction book, *Something Fierce: Memoirs of a Revolutionary Daughter*, was published in 2011 and nominated for British Columbia's National Award for Canadian Non-Fiction, the international Charles Taylor Prize for Literary Non-Fiction, the 2012 BC Book Prize, and won CBC Canada Reads 2012. Aguirre has more than sixty film, TV, and stage acting credits, is a Theatre of the Oppressed workshop facilitator, and an instructor in the acting department at Vancouver Film School. Aguirre is a graduate of Studio 58.

Set in a run-down hotel in 1974, only months after the start of the infamous Pinochet regime, eight Chilean refugees struggle, at times haplessly, at times profoundly, to decide if seeing their homeland means they have abandoned their friends and responsibilities or not. More than a dark comedy about a group of Chilean refugees who arrive in Vancouver after Pinochet's coup, this play is an attempt to give voice to refugee communities from all corners of the globe.

The Refugee Hotel was first produced by Alameda Theatre Company in association with Theatre Passe Muraille and premiered at Theatre Passe Muraille, Toronto, on September 16, 2009.

* * *

CALLADITA, FLACA, FAT JORGE, CRISTINA, JOSELITO, MANUELITA, and MANUEL descend the stairs. MANUEL is aided by the cueca dancer, who is invisible to everyone else.

FLACA: *(to MANUEL)* Need any help?

MANUEL shakes his head no.

MANUELITA: I bet there's finally a letter from Grandma.

JOSELITO: I don't see why we have to check the mail every day. It'll take a month for a letter to get here.

FLACA: Because it's a ritual. And those are important.

MANUELITA: Uncle Manuel, can I hold your hand?

MANUEL nods.

BILL O'Neill enters. He is drenched.

JOSELITO: Hey! *(pointing at BILL)* Look at that hippie!

FLACA: *(to JOSELITO)* Don't point.

BILL: How beauty to look you! Me can't believe this! Me feel like I'm in Chile once more!

MANUELITA: You're not. You're in Canada.

FAT JORGE: I can't believe it! I can't believe it! You're the first gringo we meet here who speaks Spanish and there's so many things we need to talk about, comrade.

BILL: (*to the Chileans*) Me Bill. Just got back of Santiago. Hear me, me spend four weeks on the National Stadium and then four weeks on Chile Stadium—

CRISTINA: Shit.

BILL: Shit is correct. Me thumb, uh, climb?

CRISTINA: Hitchhike!

BILL: Yes. Yes. Hitchhike. South America. Hitchhike Chile as coup take place. Arrested for long hair and beard. Fifty-six days in camps of concentrations and me learn that life is intense, precious, like jewel.

I find out you chilis here and I come down to look at you immediately. Me want to let you understand that many, many gringos in solidarity with you chilis and we provide couches—no, um, support—anything you desire. Not just gringos. The Palestinians wants express their fraternal hellos—

MANUEL: Did you see Galindo Rodríguez in Chile Stadium?

BILL: Uh—

MANUEL: What about Carmen Rojas?

BILL: Okay, me look at too many people—

MANUEL: You must have seen Emilio Moreno and his wife Matilde—

BILL: That names sound familiars, but me has very many names on my head, you understand—

MANUEL: I just want to know if they're still alive, or what happened to them—

FLACA: Calm down, Manuel. The poor man has just arrived and we haven't even offered him a seat.

CRISTINA puts her hand on MANUEL's back and rubs it.

BILL: No, no. Me understand. Me assemble list with help of Interfaith Church, they wants get people out of Chile soon possible, you have names to sprinkle on list?—

FLACA: Please, sit down. Make yourself at home.

BILL: Hear me, me acquire name of government workperson on your case. Me investigate your situation. Me inform you.

FAT JORGE: All I know is that this is a hotel we're staying in and I know that hotels are expensive. I've never stayed in a hotel. Ever in my life. And now here we are for five nights already and we don't have a penny to pay for it. So we've been looking for jobs, but to no avail—

BILL: Oh, God me. You NO PAY for hotel—

JOSELITO: Told ya!

BILL: Don't be nervous. Me speak on the worker. Me speak on the receptionist and inform you.

BILL opens his backpack and starts pulling out a bottle of wine.

But right now, time celebrate our arrival on Canada. Look me!

CRISTINA: Wine!

BILL: Yes. Come join us. No Chilean however. We boycott Chilean wine, correct?

FAT JORGE: Of course, comrade.

BILL: Italian.

The receptionist brings glasses. BILL pours the wine for everybody.

I'll get the kids some pop.

BILL buys two Cokes from the vending machine.

FAT JORGE: So that's how the stupid thing works! Shoulda known. You have to pay for everything in this country. Capitalism is—

FLACA: Fat Jorge, don't start with one of your speeches.

(to BILL) You have to forgive him. You see, his conscience was born in prison, and now he has to keep trying it out all the time.

BILL: Me. I the same.

FLACA and BILL share a look.

You are Camila Urrutia?

FLACA: Yes, I am.

BILL: Oh, God me. You're . . . *(choosing his words carefully, aware that her children are in the room)* You're . . . well, you be example. There be many stories about you in the prisoners. You know, about the pain you endure and in spite you keep all information inside, give nobody away . . . You resistance symbol . . . Excuse me: you not be executed one week ago?

FLACA: I was headed for the firing squad with the nine others and then all of a sudden the blindfold gets taken off and I'm loaded into a Canadian embassy car, driven for eighteen hours straight to Santiago airport, taken to a plane, and handcuffed.

FAT JORGE: We were waiting to enter the plane, where she was supposed to be waiting for us, but I never thought it was true.

FLACA: And then there they all were. Walking down the aisle. My kids were so big and my husband was almost skinny!

MANUELITA: He's always throwing up.

JOSELITO: Shhhh.

BILL: Oh, comrades. My heart is big with you. (*holding up his drink*) Me want welcome you chilis to Canada, my country. Me toast you for survive, for come here, for enrich my country with your wisdom. Me want you stay on many years, but me hopes that Pinochet fall and you return your homeland much sooner than later!

FAT JORGE: A toast! To us, to you, to the old gringo, to the refugee hotel!

They all drink.

CRISTINA: (*to MANUEL, intimately*) And to you, the martyr of Dawson Island.

ANUSREE ROY
TRIDENT MOON

Anusree Roy is a Governor General's Literary Award nominated–
writer and an actor whose work has premiered internationally. Her
plays include *Little Pretty and the Exceptional*, *Trident Moon*, *Sultans of
the Street*, *Brothel #9*, *Roshni*, *Letters to my Grandma*, and *Pyaasa*. She
holds a master's degree from the University to Toronto and has been
published by Playwrights Canada Press. Her plays and performances
have won her four Dora Mavor Moore Awards, and she is the recipient of the K.M. Hunter Artist Award, RBC Emerging Artist Award,
Carol Bolt Award, and Siminovitch Protégé Prize and was a finalist for
the Susan Smith Blackburn Prize.

Six women, three Muslim and three Hindu, hide inside a coal truck as
it speeds through the newly divided Hindustan in 1947. Nothing will
prevent Alia getting to West Bengal. Her former employers are now
her captives and she will have revenge for what they have done, even
if she has to harm the child she has spent her life raising. Violence
and hatred threaten to engulf those inside the truck, but when it suddenly stops, the women must find what unites them in order to have
any chance of survival.

Trident Moon was first produced by Finborough Theatre, London,
England, on October 9, 2016.

* * *

As ALIA undoes her bandages, takes dirt from the pouch, and applies it to BANI's gunshot wound, RANI and PAKHI stare at BANI.

BANI: What you both staring at? Never seen anyone dying before?

ALIA: You not dying.

Beat.

BANI: (*to PAKHI and RANI*) My sister do servant work in your house for so long, how Kabir and me never meet you all before today, hai?

Beat.

(*to PAKHI*) My dead brother-in-law teach you to drive?

Pause. PAKHI just stares.

BANI: Hai?

No answer.

ALIA: Of course he teach her how to drive. How she learn so good otherwise.

Slight pause. ALIA continues the bandaging.

BANI: (*to PAKHI*) Why that Aasim marry you when he already having this ugly one?

Pause.

Huh?

ALIA: *(relishing it)* Because she so ugly. The other servants in the house say to me that they hear rumour that Rani Madam hole so tight Aasim SirJi could never go in. *(indicating Pakhi)* So he got this new one. He call her his *peacock*.

RANI gives her a sharp look.

RANI: You lying shit. God is listening—

ALIA: You know it's true. Rani Madam had hair down to her knees, and the day Aasim SirJi got his pretty peacock Pakhi bride she chop it all off.

BANI: Tight hole, that hair and ugly face—no one loves you, no?

HEERA: *(touching her crotch)* I am have to go.

PAKHI: Hold it.

HEERA: I am not be—

PAKHI: Hold it.

ALIA: *(to HEERA)* What I am teach you, take deep breath and think of something else. Do it, Janu—

HEERA: Mummy—

PAKHI: Shh . . .

ALIA: Do it, take a deep breath—

The women are suddenly aware that the truck is gradually slowing down. As this happens sounds such as "Pakistan Zindabad" become more prominent and audible.

BANI: Why is he slow down?

ALIA knocks on the front of the truck and whispers.

ALIA: Kabir, what is matter? Military?

ALIA listens.

Kabir. You hear me?

Muffled through the cab, KABIR speaks to ALIA.

BANI: Listen to what he say—

ALIA: I am not hear—

BANI: Listen harder—

Outside, the rioting sounds become more prominent. People screaming. Sounds of chaos.

ALIA grabs ARUN and puts her hand on ARUN's mouth. ARUN struggles.

The truck has completely stopped.

ALIA: Quiet Arun! Kabir . . . you can hear me? Don't stop!

BANI: (*to ARUN*) Shh . . . everything be okay—

ALIA: Don't stop, Kabir!—

BANI: Listen harder!

KABIR speaks, still muffled.

HEERA: (*continuous overlap*) Mumma?—

RANI: Hold still—

PAKHI: Oh God oh God oh God—

There is a heightened sense of angst inside the truck. Suddenly there is loud banging on the side of the truck. The banging stops. The women look at each other.

Silence for a beat.

Suddenly more loud banging.

Beat.

No one knows what to do. ALIA tries to hide PAKHI, RANI, and HEERA.

There is nowhere to hide them.

She covers BANI's gunshot wound/blood, etc. Suddenly PAKHI starts to scream. RANI joins mid-scream.

HELP US! WOMEN IN HERE. HELP HELP—

RANI: (*to HEERA*) Bang the truck. Bang. Scream, Heera!

HEERA starts to bang the side of the truck with all her might.

PAKHI & RANI: HELP! WE BEING ABDUCTED. HELP! MUSLIM BROTHERS, LISTEN!

As the above happens, ALIA overturns a bucket of pumpkin and rice and pulls out a small handgun and points it at them. Sudden stillness.

Beat.

ALIA: (*to RANI and PAKHI*) Shut it right now you both! You forget I am have a gun? It could be anyone outside who wanting to kill us all!

(*speaks towards KABIR*) What is happen? Kabir?—

ARUN: Who is there?—

ALIA: (*sharp*) Shhh!—

KABIR speaks, muffled. Loud banging from outside. ALIA goes toward the door.

ALIA: (*loud, authoritative*) Who is bang? We have a gun—

BANI: (*to ALIA, whispering*) And . . . knives and big guns and bombs—

ALIA: (*loud, authoritative*) And knives and guns. Big big guns and bombs—

Beat. The muffled sounds come closer. A heavily pregnant woman, SONALI, appears. She is holding a small cloth sack that contains

*her belongings. She is wearing a Bengali style Salwar kameez.
The dupatta covers her head. Beside her is an older Indian temple
priest holding an axe. They are both anxiously looking around,
making sure they don't get caught. They both come to the side of
the truck.*

SONALI: *(whispers)* Open. Open, sister, please. Open.

ALIA: Who is it?

ARUN: *(overlap)* Who is it?

SONALI: Me. It's me. I . . . Sonali. I having babies . . . inside me. Please helping. The man say to me to say to you to open.

BANI: *(to ALIA)* Which man?

ALIA: Which man?

SONALI: Driving man. He says to open. I am giving him all the money we are having and a gold coin—

BANI: This greedy man . . . he is stopping to pick up for money! He will get us killed—

ALIA: *(to KABIR)* Kabir! Don't change the plan!—

PAKHI: Don't get in! They are abducting us! Get help—

HEERA: *(continuous overlap)* Mumma?

SONALI: I am *need* help—

ALIA: (*to BANI*) Should I open?—

BANI: NO, wait, what if Kabir on gun point and she lying—

BANI: (*to ALIA*) Ask, ask her guns—

ALIA: (*to SONALI*) How many guns you have?—

SONALI: No . . . babies—

ALIA: DON'T LIE!—

ARUN: Don't lie!—

SONALI: No, please. Please. Just babies inside my stomach. I am needing help. Driving man—

ALIA: —say you are Hindu—

(*to SONALI*) Shut up!

BANI: Kabir, you fool!

(*to ALIA*) Alone?

ALIA: (*to SONALI*) You alone?

SONALI: Yes . . . No. Only . . . the . . . my my temple priest. He is good man. He . . . he helping—

ALIA: If you are lying, I am kill you as soon as I am see you—

PAKHI: How can you trust her—

BANI: Wait, wait . . . tell her . . . ask her to . . . ask her to ask Kabir what is in the bucket . . . if he answer wrong on purpose then we know he is trouble.

ALIA: (*to SONALI*) Go . . . go ask the driving man what is in the bucket.

SONALI: What?

ALIA: Man. The driving man, go ask him what is in the bucket—

SONALI: Sister, why you are wasting time—

ALIA: DO IT!

> *They disappear. Silence inside the truck. A sharp contrast to the intense riot sounds outside. They appear again.*

SONALI: A pumpkin, rice, and dirt.

ALIA: (*to BANI, whispering*) Safe.

BANI: Kabir, you fool you fool you fool . . . let her in.

> *SONALI looks at the priest.*

PRIEST: This is good . . . it be good.

> *Beat.*

> *ALIA looks at BANI.*

> *Beat.*

ALIA unlocks the truck door. As soon as ALIA sees them, she points the gun at them.

SONALI: (*to ALIA*) No no no no, don't kill. We Hindu! I am swear of Ma Durga. Look, he be priest. Look, white thread.

(*to the priest*) Show, show, show thread.

The priest pulls out a white thread from underneath his shirt.

ALIA: (*scans the outside really fast*) What do you want?

SONALI: Please please please . . . help us, help us. Please. This is totally Muslim area now. They are forcing all Hindu women whose husband gone missing to jump and drown inside the well so Muslim men not raping. My own father trying to throw me in. This good man, this man helping me. He my temple priest. (*touches her stomach*) I am having two inside here. The new country border is not that far. I am—

RANI: (*panicked*) Listen, do not get in! This one is our dirty Hindu servant. Eating our food for years and now abducting my family. These are killer! / Get us help!—

PAKHI: We need to get out! Help us!—

ALIA: (*pointing gun at RANI and PAKHI*) Shut it!—

BANI: (*from inside the truck, to ALIA*) How much money did she give Kabir?

ALIA: (*to SONALI*) How much money did you give my brother-in-law?

SONALI: Everything, sister. All the money and my only gold coin. Please. Let me in—

PAKHI: (*continuous overlap*) Help us, please please—

ALIA: How I know you Hindu?—

PRIEST: She is, I am seeing her since childhood, she—

RANI: HELP US! Please—

ALIA: Quiet!

PRIEST: She is innocent girl! God will—

RANI: HELP, please!—

ALIA: QUIET, I SAID!

SONALI: I am . . . ask me anything. Any song. We know Lord Shiva prayer, Laxmi song, Durga prayer . . . anything. Which one? Anyone?

PAKHI: (*to SONALI, yelling from inside to the truck*) Don't . . . don't trust / this one.

ALIA: Shut it—

PAKHI: She is killer. Please / help.

ALIA: Shut it, I / said—

RANI: She is killer—

PAKHI: She kill our husband Aasim and now forcing us . . . don't trust this one.

> *Suddenly, in close proximity, a number of gunshots are heard, along with an explosion.* ALIA *goes to close the door.*

AHMED GHAZALI, TRANSLATED BY BOBBY THEODORE
THE SHEEP AND THE WHALE
/ LE MOUTON ET LA BALEINE

Moroccan Canadian Ahmed Ghazali is an expert in cultural engineering. He has lived in Casablanca, Paris, and Montreal, and since 2004, in Barcelona. He is Director of the company K.NOUR, dedicated to the design and construction of museums and exhibitions. He is also a playwright. His plays have been translated into several languages and widely staged in different countries. Among his plays are *The Sheep and the Whale* (Editions théâtrales, Paris, 2002) and *Timbuktu, 52 Days by Camel* (Icaria, Barcelona, 2005). He is the winner of the SACD Award (2002).

Bobby Theodore is a screenwriter, playwright, and translator. He has worked on several TV series, including *Murdoch Mysteries*, *Flashpoint*, and *Knuckleheads,* and he wrote for the acclaimed CBC radio drama, *Afghanada*. Nominated for a Governor General's Literary Award in 2000 for his translation of *15 Seconds* by François Archambault, Bobby has now translated over thirty plays from French to English. For the stage, Bobby co-created *300 Tapes* (with Ame Henderson). In 2014, his translation of François Archambault's *You Will Remember Me* premiered at ATP, won a Betty Mitchell Award for Outstanding New Play, and was produced across Canada and in the USA.

In a series of unforgettable images, a freighter in the Strait of Gibraltar seeks to unload its shipment of unwanted cargo, a stowaway embarks on a dangerous passage, and a couple's love is suspended between two worlds.

The Sheep and the Whale was first produced in English by Cahoots Theatre, Modern Times Stage Company, and Theatre Passe Muraille, Toronto, from February 13, 2007 to March 11, 2007.

Le Mouton et la baleine premiered at Théâtre de Quat'sous, Montreal, on January 15, 2001.

* * *

One a.m. During a violent storm in the Strait of Gibraltar, a cargo ship pitches and reels in the swell. A rescue operation is underway. A small craft containing Moroccan illegal immigrants has sunk and the sailors are trying to save the shipwrecked. There's much excitement on deck: screams of the drowning, deafening wail of sirens, sailors' shouts as they run around the ship. Violent waves pound the deck, strong gusts from the storm . . . Fog and flashing lights, alarms sounding. Sailors bring in the bodies of the drowned one by one and leave them in the middle of the deck. A man wearing a cap is on his knees, examining the bodies: the ship's DOCTOR. The following action takes place in three areas:

On the main deck, sailors, under the direction of THE FIRST MATE, lay out the bodies they've fished out of the water for THE DOCTOR to examine.

Near the compartments, CAPTAIN ROGACHEV attempts to radio neighbouring ports.

Throughout the scene, in the background, we hear the harrowing screams of the drowning coming all the way from the sea: Help! Save me! النجدة!

THE DOCTOR: They're all dead!

CAPTAIN ROGACHEV: *(to the radio)* Hello! Gibraltar? Hello! Gibraltar?

THE FIRST MATE: *(to sailors who bring in a* SURVIVOR*)* Bring him over here!

CAPTAIN ROGACHEV: Hello! Gibraltar? Good morning, Gibraltar! This is Captain Rogachev of the *Caucasus*, a Russian freighter. We are four miles from Gibraltar. A boat just sank in my course and we've fished the bodies . . . what? Yes, it is a tragedy . . .

THE FIRST MATE: *(to the* SURVIVOR*)* Where are you from?

CAPTAIN ROGACHEV: What I am asking, sir, is for permission to bring the bodies in before continuing on my way . . . What? It's not your problem? You're not supposed to be here . . . I see. Then who should I talk to? I have to bring these bodies in . . .

Sailors carry more bodies in for THE DOCTOR *to examine.*

What? We have to ask the others? What others? I see . . . Thank you, sir . . . Good night, sir.

He ends the radio conversation and turns toward the others.

Not his problem, he says. The English aren't supposed to be in the Strait, he says. They only have visitor status in Gibraltar. An historical exception, he says.

THE DOCTOR: This one is still alive.

He grabs a sailor.

Come on! Help me!

SAILOR #2: What?

THE DOCTOR: Get on your knees!

CAPTAIN ROGACHEV: Hello! Algeciras? Hello! Spania! Do you read me?

SAILOR #2: *(to THE DOCTOR)* What!?

THE DOCTOR: Get on your knees, damn it! Blow hard into his mouth when I tell you.

THE DOCTOR starts pressing down on the drowning victim's chest frantically.

Okay, now!

SAILOR #2: What?

CAPTAIN ROGACHEV: *(to the others)* Quiet!

(into the radio) Hello! Algeciras? Hello! Spania!

THE DOCTOR: Blow into his mouth, for God's sake!

The sailor blows on the man's mouth from a distance, like it's a candle. Enraged, THE DOCTOR pushes the sailor out of the way. THE DOCTOR begins to do both actions himself.

CAPTAIN ROGACHEV: (*into the radio*) Hello! Algeciras, hello! Spania! Spania! Do you read me? Buenos dias, Algeciras. This is Captain Rogachev of the *Caucasus* . . . We are in the middle of the Strait of Gibraltar, a few miles from Algeciras . . .

THE DOCTOR: (*realizing the man is dead*) Goddamn it!

CAPTAIN ROGACHEV: (*into the radio*) A boat sank in our course. I've pulled out some drowned men . . . bodies. What? Hold on, one moment, por favor.

(*to the others*) How many are there?

THE FIRST MATE: What?

CAPTAIN ROGACHEV: How many bodies are there!?

THE FIRST MATE: I don't know!

CAPTAIN ROGACHEV: Count them, goddamn it!

THE DOCTOR: Nine! No . . . ten! There's ten.

CAPTAIN ROGACHEV: (*into the radio*) Ten bodies, señor, and one survivor . . . what? I don't know, señor. How am I supposed to know where they're from? What? You want me to see if they're what?

He bursts out laughing.

One moment, por favor . . .

(*to the others*) Hey! Are they circumcised?

THE FIRST MATE: What?

Losing patience, CAPTAIN ROGACHEV *grabs his crotch.*

CAPTAIN ROGACHEV: See if they're circumcised!

THE DOCTOR: *(to* CAPTAIN ROGACHEV*)* They are.

CAPTAIN ROGACHEV: Si, señor, they're circumcised . . . You're saying that's normal . . . It happens all the time . . . I see . . . El problema, señor, is that I would like to bring you these bodies and get on my way . . . Sorry? . . . It's not your problem . . . I have to talk to the others . . . what others? I see . . . Gracias, señor . . . Buenas noches, señor!

(to the others) He says it's not his problem. They're illegals, Arabs, Africans. He says it's been like this for centuries with the Moors. He says Spain is sick of taking it up the ass for Europe.

THE FIRST MATE shouts at the SURVIVOR, *who is screaming, in a state of shock.*

THE FIRST MATE: Shut your mouth!

THE FIRST MATE slaps him.

Shut up!

CAPTAIN ROGACHEV: *(into the radio)* Hello! Tangiers? Hello! Tangiers?

Intervening, THE DOCTOR *pushes* THE FIRST MATE *away.*

THE DOCTOR: What's the matter with you? Can't you see he's in shock?

CAPTAIN ROGACHEV: Hello Morocco! Hello Tangiers! Can you read me? Salamalec Tangiers. This is Captain Rogachev aboard the *Caucasus* . . . a Russian freighter . . . Russian! We're in the Strait of Gibraltar a few miles from Tangiers . . . We've just . . . You're right, it is late . . . Right—one in the morning . . .

THE DOCTOR: (*to the* SURVIVOR *as he examines him*) Calm down! It's going to be all right.

CAPTAIN ROGACHEV: (*into the radio*) No sir, I don't want to enter Tangiers, my destination is Marseilles . . . What? No, no . . . It's just that . . . let me talk and you'll understand, we've come from the Gulf of Guinea and we're heading to Marseilles. Now we're in the Strait of Gibraltar, a few miles from Tangiers and we've just . . . what? Right, we don't have the right to enter the port, that's true, but . . . hello Tangiers! Hello Tangiers!

SAILOR #1: (*to* THE FIRST MATE) There's some more that got swept away by the current, boss!

THE DOCTOR: We have to lower the lifeboats!

THE FIRST MATE: No!

CAPTAIN ROGACHEV: (*into the radio*) Yes, I know, port taxes.

THE DOCTOR *runs to the rails and looks over.*

THE DOCTOR: We can't let them drown!

CAPTAIN ROGACHEV: (*into the radio*) But I'm not asking for entry to the port, sir.

THE FIRST MATE: (*to THE DOCTOR*) I'm not the Red Cross!

CAPTAIN ROGACHEV: I'm notifying you that we've just fished out some bod— . . . No, I'm not talking about fishing! Hello Tangiers! Hello Tangiers! Yes, I know . . . it's forbidden to fish here . . . right . . . yes, there's no more fish, Europe wiped everything out . . . I see . . . Yes, actually, it is depressing . . . But sir, I'm not talking about fish . . . We fished out *bodies*, drowned, illegals, your fellow countrymen sir . . . Ten . . . Hello Tangiers! Can you read me? Hello Tangiers!

THE DOCTOR: (*to the SURVIVOR*) How many others were on the boat?

CAPTAIN ROGACHEV: I want to bring you the bodies before getting back on course . . . Inshallah? What does that mean? I'm telling you that . . . Sorry? A holiday? What feast? What are you talking about? I have bodies here . . . what? Sheep? Sheep? Hello! Tangiers! Hello! Tangiers!

The connection is cut. Stunned, he turns toward the others.

Sheep?! He said—sheep!

Blackout.

* * *

Une heure du matin. Une tempête violente dans le détroit de Gibraltar. Le cargo tangue sur la houle. Une opération de sauvetage est en cours. Une embarcation de clandestins marocains vient de sombrer dans le détroit. On tente de sauver les naufragés. Le pont est très agité: cris des noyés, bruit assourdissant des sirènes, cris et pas des marins qui courent. Clapotis violents des flots sur le pont et rafales de la tempête. Brouillard et lumières étincelantes, signaux d'alarme. Des marins ramènent au fur et à mesure les corps des noyés qu'ils déposent au milieu du pont. Un homme qui porte une casquette est à genoux en train d'examiner les cadavres: c'est LE MÉDECIN *du bord. L'action se passe en trois lieux différents:*

— sur le pont principal, les marins, dirigés par LE SECOND, *déposent les cadavres repêchés que* LE MÉDECIN *examine;*

— près des cabines, le CAPITAINE ROGATCHEV *est en communication radio avec les ports voisins;*

Pendant toute la scène, on entend en bruit de fond les cris déchirants des noyés depuis la mer: Au secours! À moi! النجدة!

LE MÉDECIN: Ils sont tous morts!

CAPITAINE ROGATCHEV: *(à la radio)* Allô! Gibraltar! Allô! Gibraltar!

LE SECOND: *(aux marins qui ramènent un* SURVIVANT) Ici! Amenez-le ici!

CAPITAINE ROGATCHEV: Allô! Gibraltar? Good morning, Gibraltar! Capitaine Rogatchev sur le *Caucase*, un cargo russe. Nous sommes à quatre milles de Gibraltar. Une barque vient de sombrer sur mon parcours et nous venons de repêcher à l'instant des cadavres . . . What? C'est tragique en effet, yes . . .

LE SECOND: (*au* SURVIVANT) D'où vous venez?

CAPITAINE ROGATCHEV: The question, sir, est que je voudrais livrer ces corps avant de poursuivre ma route . . . Pardon? It is not your problem? You're not supposed to be here . . . I see . . . À qui je dois m'adresser alors? Je dois quand même livrer ces corps . . .

> Les marins amènent d'autres corps que LE MÉDECIN examine.

What? Il faut voir avec les autres? Qui sont les autres? I see . . . Thank you, sir . . . Good night, sir. (*fin de communication,* CAPITAINE ROGATCHEV *se tourne vers les autres*) Ce n'est pas son problème, il dit. Les Anglais ne sont pas supposés être dans le détroit, il dit. Ils sont là à titre de visiteurs seulement. Un état d'exception historique, il dit.

LE MÉDECIN: Celui-là vit encore! (*attrape un marin*) Viens! Aide-moi!

DEUXIÈME MARIN: Comment!?

LE MÉDECIN: À genoux!

CAPITAINE ROGATCHEV: (*à la radio*) Allô! Algésiras! Allô! Spania! Vous m'en tendez?

DEUXIÈME MARIN: (*au* MÉDECIN) Quoi!?

LE MÉDECIN: (*au* DEUXIÈME MARIN) Tombe à genoux, bordel, et souffle fort dans sa bouche quand je te le dis!

> LE MÉDECIN *se met à presser le corps de la victime avec un geste frénétique.*

Maintenant!

DEUXIÈME MARIN: Quoi!?

CAPITAINE ROGATCHEV: (*aux autres*) Taisez-vous! (*à la radio*) Allô! Algésiras! Allô! Spania!

LE MÉDECIN: (*au DEUXIÈME MARIN*) Souffle dans sa bouche, nom de Dieu!

> *Le marin souffle sur la bouche, à distance, comme sur une bougie. Fou de rage, LE MÉDECIN le repousse, le renverse loin du corps et se met à faire lui-même les deux opérations.*

CAPITAINE ROGATCHEV: Allô! Algésiras! Allô! Spania! Spania! Vous m'entendez? Buenos dias, Algésiras. Capitaine Rogatchev sur le *Caucase* . . . Nous sommes au milieu du détroit de Gibraltar, à quelques milles d'Algésiras . . .

LE MÉDECIN: (*réalise que la victime vient d'expirer*) Merde!

CAPITAINE ROGATCHEV: (*à la radio*) Une barque vient de sombrer sur mon parcours, j'ai repêché des noyés . . . Pardon? Un instant, por favor. (*aux autres*) Combien ils sont?

LE SECOND: (*au CAPITAINE ROGATCHEV*) Quoi?

CAPITAINE ROGATCHEV: (*au SECOND*) Combien il y a de corps là?

LE SECOND: (*au CAPITAINE ROGATCHEV*) J'en sais rien, moi!

CAPITAINE ROGATCHEV: (*au SECOND*) Compte-les, bordel!

LE MÉDECIN: (*au CAPITAINE ROGATCHEV*) Neuf! Non, dix! Ils sont dix.

CAPITAINE ROGATCHEV: (*à la radio*) Dix corps, señor, et un survivant . . . Comment? Je ne sais pas, señor, comment est-ce que je peux savoir d'où ils viennent? Pardon? Vous voulez que je regarde si . . . (*éclate de rire*) Un moment, por favor. (*aux autres*) Est-ce qu'ils sont circoncis?

LE SECOND: (*au CAPITAINE ROGATCHEV*) Quoi!?

CAPITAINE ROGATCHEV: (*impatient, tape sur son sexe*) Regarde s'ils sont circoncis!

LE MÉDECIN: (*au CAPITAINE ROGATCHEV*) Ils le sont!

    Éclat de rire des marins.

CAPITAINE ROGATCHEV: Si, señor, ils sont circoncis . . . C'est normal, vous dites . . . Ça arrive tout le temps . . . Je vois . . . El problema, señor, est que je voudrais vous livrer ces corps avant de poursuivre mon chemin . . . Pardon? Ce n'est pas votre problème . . . Il faut voir avec les autres . . . Oui sont les autres? Je vois . . . Gracias, señor! Buenas noches, señor. (*Fin de communication. Aux autres.*) Ce n'est pas son problème, il dit. Ce sont des clandestins, des Arabes, des Africains. C'est comme ça depuis des siècles avec les Maures, il dit. L'Espagne en a ras le cul d'être le cul de l'Europe, il dit.

LE SECOND: (*au SURVIVANT qui, en état de choc, se met à hurler*) Ta gueule! (*lui donne une gifle*) La ferme!

CAPITAINE ROGATCHEV: (*à la radio*) Allô! Tanger! Allô! Tanger!

LE MÉDECIN: (*s'interpose et repousse LE SECOND*) Qu'est-ce qui te prend? Tu vois pas qu'il est en état de choc?

CAPITAINE ROGATCHEV: Allô, Maroc! Allô, Tanger! Vous m'entendez? Salamalec, Tanger. Capitaine Rogatchev sur le *Caucase*... Un cargo russe... Russe! Nous sommes dans le détroit de Gibraltar, à quelques milles de Tanger... Nous venons de... Oui, il est tard, en effet... Une heure du matin, c'est ça...

LE MÉDECIN: (*au* SURVIVANT *qu'il examine*) Calme-toi! Ça va aller!

CAPITAINE ROGATCHEV: Non, monsieur, je ne désire pas entrer à Tanger, ma destination c'est Marseille... Comment? Non, non... C'est que... Laissez-moi parler et vous allez tout comprendre... Nous venons du golfe de Guinée et nous nous dirigeons vers Marseille et là nous sommes dans le détroit de Gibraltar, juste à quelques milles de Tanger et nous venons de... Comment? Oui, nous n'avons pas le droit d'entrer au port, c'est exact... Allô, Tanger! Allô, Tanger!

PREMIER MARIN: (*au* SECOND) Il y en a d'autres qui sont portés loin par le courant, chef!

LE MÉDECIN: Il faut descendre les canots de sauvetage!

LE SECOND: (*au* MÉDECIN) Pas question!

CAPITAINE ROGATCHEV: (*à la radio*) Oui, les taxes portuaires, je sais...

LE MÉDECIN: (*court au bastingage et regarde*) Nous n'allons pas les laisser se noyer!

CAPITAINE ROGATCHEV: (*à la radio*) Mais, monsieur, ce n'est pas l'accès au port que je vous demande...

LE SECOND: (*au* MÉDECIN) Je ne suis pas la Croix-Rouge!

CAPITAINE ROGATCHEV: (*à la radio*) C'est pour vous signaler que nous venons à l'inslant de repêcher des cad... Je ne vous parle pas de pêcher des poissons! Allô, Tanger! Allô, Tanger!... Oui, c'est ça, interdit de pêcher ici... Il n'y a plus de poissons, vous dites? L'Europe a toul raflé... Je vois... C'est désolant, en effet... Mais, monsieur, je ne vous parle pas de poissons, ce sont des cadavres que nous venons de repêcher à l'instant, des noyés, des clandestins, vos compatriotes, monsieur... Dix... Allô, Tanger! Vous m'entendez? Allô, Tanger!

LE MÉDECIN: (*au SURVIVANT*) Combien vous étiez sur la barque?

CAPITAINE ROGATCHEV: La question, monsieur, est que je voudrais vous remettre les corps avant de poursuivre ma roule... Inchallah, vous dites? Qu'est-ce que ça veut dire?... Mais, monsieur, je vous dis que... Pardon? C'est la fête? De quelle fête vous me parlez, monsieur? Je vous dis que j'ai des corps ici... Pardon? Mouton? Mouton, vous dites? Allô! Tanger! Allô! Tanger!

La communication est coupée, CAPITAINE ROGATCHEV, *stupéfait, se tourne vers les autres.*

Mouton? Il a dit: «mouton»!

Noir.

SELF

DAVID YEE
PAPER SERIES

David Yee is a mixed-race (half Chinese, half Scottish) actor and playwright, born and raised in Toronto. He is the co-founding artistic director of fu-GEN Theatre Company, Canada's premiere professional Asian Canadian theatre company. A Dora Mavor Moore Award–nominated actor and playwright, his work has been produced internationally and at home. He is a two-time Governor General's Literary Award nominee for his plays *lady in the red dress* and *carried away on the crest of a wave*, which won the award in 2015 along with the Carol Bolt Award in 2013. He has worked extensively in the Asian Canadian community as an artist, advocate, and community leader. He has been called many things, but prefers "outlaw poet" to them all.

An unhappy orphan who finds solace in paper cut-outs of her parents, an Indian doctor who displays his medical degree in his taxi cab, and waiters who tamper with fortune cookies are some of the vibrant characters who are brought to life in this anthology of six monologues that revolve around paper. From drama to comedy to crime-thriller, Yee brings us a variety of plots and characters in a series of imaginative, thought-provoking vignettes.

paper SERIES was first produced by Cahoots Theatre Company at the Young Centre for the Performing Arts, Toronto, between March 18 and April 9, 2011.

* * *

We are in MUTT'S *bedroom.* MUTT *is a girl of about eight years. She has a plethora of stuffed animals in her room, propped up as an audience, and a small cut-out cardboard box on a stand that serves for putting on puppet shows. There is a small table next to it that has several sheets of paper, markers, scissors, and other various items lying on it.* MUTT *comes in, slamming the door behind her and yelling defiantly:*

MUTT: *Well I don't even like your dinner, so* BLEH!

She sits down at the table and scowls, then sets to work cutting crude figures out of paper. She stands them up, two crude puppets, one male and one female.

(as female) Blah blah blah me me me . . .

(as male) Blah blah blah you you you . . .

(as both) Go to your room for no reason! No dinner!

Pause.

Blah!

MUTT *looks up at the audience of stuffed animals.*

My new parents. The Blahs. *(indicates the female)* Mrs. Blah. *(indicates the male)* And Mr. Blah.

Deviously, she picks up a marker and draws on Mr. Blah's face.

Mr. Blah has one big eyebrow instead of two. He wears big ugly glasses and smells like envelopes.

She draws Mrs. Blah.

Mrs. Blah has big fake boobs and looks kind of like a racoon.

She picks up the scissors and waves them toward the Blahs.

(*as the Blahs*) Noooooooooo!!!!!!!!!!!

She snips their heads off and happily discards the bodies.

I heard them talking. They're going to give me back in the morning. This is my fifth family this year. Sister Sheila says God is punishing me. She says that's what God does to people like me. Mutts. She says that this is what happens when people crossbreed coloured people and white people. No one wants us.

Pause.

Sister Sheila says if I was one or the other, then I'd find a family. Mutts just get traded like baseball cards.

MUTT sits at the desk and searches for something. She can't find it. She does another tour of the room but comes up empty. She looks at her stuffed animal audience.

Have you guys seen my real parents?

Pause.

The Blahs threw them out, didn't they?

Pause.

Yeah, thought so. Oh well. We can make them again.

She takes some paper and scissors and goes to work. She cuts two paper figures and starts colouring them in, narrating as she goes.

My father was Scottish. Scottish people play soccer, but they call it football, and eat things like sheep guts.

She continues making the figures.

They drink lots of beer and talk with funny accents.

She completes her father. Continues making her mother.

Mom was "Oriental." They all eat rice and talk with funny accents and are very very polite and good at math.

She finishes making her mother.

Hi guys.

FATHER: Right, hallo, wee lassie!

MOTHER: Konnichi-wa. Ne ho mah!

She looks at her paper parents with pleasure, and a little bit of sadness.

MUTT: I never met them. But I think they looked like this.

Pause.

I miss you guys.

MOTHER: (*weakly*) We missing you too . . .

MUTT is despondent.

MUTT: Forget it . . .

She folds her arms and lays her head down. Her parents are now on either side of her.

MOTHER: She sounding upset.

FATHER: Poor lass.

MOTHER: She grow up be so pretty.

FATHER: (*flirtatious*) Aye, just like her mother.

MOTHER laughs timidly . . . actually, everything she does is timid.

MOTHER: Oh, stop . . . leng jai-ah.

They kiss, MOTHER squeals . . . timidly.

FATHER: Shhh. You'll wake her up!

MUTT sits up.

MUTT: I'm not sleeping. Are you guys coming back soon?

FATHER: We're here now, lass.

MUTT: But the real you. The one without a Popsicle stick holding you up. Can you come get me? I hate it here.

MOTHER: You need cheering up. I make you some congee.

MUTT: What's congee?

MOTHER: (*shocked*) What? No one ever make you congee! What sort of place you live in?

FATHER: Calm down, missus. She dinnae need porridge anyway. I can cheer her up with my remarkable Sean Connery impression. (*imitates Sean Connery*) Mishter Goldfinger, I preshume.

He looks to MOTHER *and* MUTT *for approval.*

Eh? Eh?

MUTT: Who's Sean Connery?

FATHER: (*enraged*) *What*!?! You don't know who Sean Connery is? Unacceptable!

MOTHER: Now who getting upset?

FATHER: But it's *Sean Connery*! He's a cultural institution!

MOTHER: So is congee.

FATHER: Now you look here—

MUTT: Stop it! I'm sorry I don't know about congee or Sean Connery, okay? I'm just a stupid mutt.

MOTHER: (*sotto*) Now look what you did.

FATHER: I'm sorry.

They kiss. Then, to MUTT:

Right then, who called you a mutt?

MUTT: Sister Sheila does. The other kids at the orphanage. They say no one wants a stupid half-breed.

MOTHER: What else did evil Sister tell you?

MUTT: She said that you're dead 'cause God punished you for making me. You guys were planning to have more mutt children and take over the world, so God struck you down with lightning.

MOTHER: What? No no no . . . we were not struck by lightning, daughter. We were struck by Toyota Prius!

MUTT: What?

MOTHER: Ironic, I know . . .

FATHER: Ach, it's true, lass. Here's what happened: Once upon a time. There was a lad and a lass named Father and Mother. When they met, they knew they were meant for one another. And one day they had a daughter . . .

A paper doll of MUTT as a newborn pops up.

Who they named Daughter . . . They lived in a lovely house in the Annex.

MUTT cuts them a house, then puts it inside the theatre. The dolls stand in front of it. MUTT is now the puppet master, behind the theatre, her head peering over.

MOTHER: I remember it bigger . . .

FATHER: (*chiding*) It's a bonnie house.

MOTHER: So Mother, Father, and Daughter live in this lovely, but slightly cramped, house and are very happy together. You even had a puppy. He was mix breed, just like you.

MUTT: A mutt.

MOTHER: No, not "mutt." Mix breed. Half and half. All the house was half and half. We have half one table, half another table, nail together, one kitchen table. Half of Mother's and half of Father's belongings all put together to make most original and beautiful house. Just like Daughter.

FATHER: One afternoon, when Daughter was only one year old, we went out for groceries in the car.

MUTT makes them a car and they get in.

Mother and Father in the front, Daughter in the child seat in the back. We were halfway between the Asian grocery store and the Scottish bakery when it hit us.

Another paper car pops up and smashes into their car.

MOTHER: Another car come, crash right into us! Aiyah! Father and Mother both perish. But Daughter, is miracle, still alive! Not one scratch!

FATHER: Aye. The next thing we know, there's this bright light—

MUTT shines a flashlight on them.

—and this big silver cloud appears—

A big silver cloud appears.

—and a voice says:

GOD: Oy! You there!

FATHER: It was God!

MUTT: God is Scottish?

FATHER: Yer damn right he is.

GOD: Oy! Yer dead. Right, on yer bike, le's go, Jimmy, line forms over 'ere.

MOTHER: But we couldn't go.

GOD: C'mon now, yer 'oldin up traffic.

FATHER: God. If I may call you God.

GOD: Me mates call me Angus.

MOTHER: We say: Angus! Please! We cannot leave Daughter. She is all alone. Who will care for her?

GOD: Well I cannae sen' ye bach. The lass dinnae ha' aunties or uncles?

MOTHER: No. She has no one but us.

GOD: Well load o' good tha' does her, yer dead!

FATHER: Please, Angus, can we no work something out?

GOD: Ach. A'right, ye daft humans.

MOTHER: And so, we all sat down and worked out a deal.

Contracts appear in their hands and they work over the details.

GOD: Okay, so I let ye stay and watch o'er her until she's . . . ten.

MOTHER: Thirty.

GOD: Fifteen.

MOTHER: Forty-two.

GOD: Twenty.

MOTHER: Deal. And we get to see her whenever we want. And protect her from bad people. And she go to college of her choice.

GOD: Okay okay okay! Anything else? Divine powers? Ability to turn water into wine?

MOTHER: She not drink. Turn her all red.

GOD: Now, in return . . . Father, ye'll play fer oor football league. We ha' tournies ev'ry Saturday against the Rangers.

FATHER: Magic.

GOD: And Mother . . .

MOTHER: I watch over Daughter. That full-time job.

GOD: A'right, then. Y'know, I dinnae see a lot of parents who love a child so much. We're about finished 'ere. I haveta get bach upstairs. Cheerio.

MOTHER: Angus!

Beat.

Daughter. She will be okay, ne?

GOD: Ach. Dinnae fache yersel, lass. She'll be just fine.

With that, the cloud disappears.

MUTT: Wow.

FATHER: Aye. We got you a good deal, lass.

MOTHER: Go to sleep now, Daughter. We make sure nothing bad happen.

FATHER: We'll be right here, watchin' over ye.

MUTT: I love you guys.

MOTHER: We love you too, Daughter. Now go sleep, or you get wrinkles when you're older.

MUTT: Okay. Good night.

MUTT goes to her bed, taking the dolls with her. She lays on her back and holds her parents up at her chest.

MOTHER: Goodnight, Daughter.

FATHER: Goodnight, sweet girl.

MUTT closes her eyes.

(*yawning*) I'm a bit tuckered out m'self. Care to join me in the boudoir?

MOTHER: (*giggling*) She will hear us! We traumatize her!

FATHER: Ach, she'll be fine. C'mon now . . .

They giggle as they disappear out of MUTT's sight.

DIONNE BRAND
THIRSTY

Dionne Brand is a renowned poet, novelist, and essayist. Her writing is notable for the beauty of its language, and for its intense engagement with issues of social justice. Her work includes ten volumes of poetry, five books of fiction, and two non-fiction works. She was the Poet Laureate of the City of Toronto from 2009 to 2012. For her contribution to literature in Canada she was made a Member of the Order of Canada in 2017. Dionne Brand became prominent first as an award-winning poet, winning the Governor General's Literary Award and the Trillium Book Prize for her volume *Land to Light On* and the Griffin Poetry Prize for her volume *Ossuaries*. Her latest works are the poetry collection *The Blue Clerk* and her novel *Theory*. She lives in Toronto and is a Professor in the School of English and Theatre Studies at the University of Guelph.

In 1978, Alan, a Black man, is killed in his Toronto home by police. For the women in his life—his widow, daughter, and mother—the memory of the event still reverberates, fresh and raw. Racial confrontation turns into tragedy, captured in the victim's dying word: "thirsty."

thirsty was first produced by the National Arts Centre, Ottawa on November 5, 2012.

* * *

Late afternoon. Music: Ornette Coleman—"Lonely Woman." Six to eight months after moving, the family has settled in as best they can. ALAN enters. GIRL is reading, CHLOE is sewing. Lights on two stations.

ALAN: *(to GIRL)* You're like your mother for that crazy music. Music supposed to have words.
And birds supposed to have wings.

My mother

> *ALAN points to CHLOE, who smiles through his speech and looks worried by the end.*

used to swim with me in the Rio Cobre
when I was in her belly
and when I was little she took me there
We would dive into the water, becoming weightless,
Some days it would rain and there would be a quiet
in the grass and trees
and we would hear colonies of insects and birds,
there was a road where I used to kick pebbles and dust
she would walk ahead of me a certain distance
and when she got to the hill she would look back for me
and I would hide in the tangle
and the thought would come over me
that there was a world without me
the road lit up with the red of the hills,
then shadowed in trees,
and I would run out quickly
in case I would disappear myself
and I would run ahead of her so she could see me . . .
You'll never be without me. Hear me? One day we'll have birds in here.
Hundreds.

GIRL: Hundreds? Papa, there's no room.

Pause.

What kind?

ALAN: All kinds, yellow and green ones.

GIRL: No, what kind, parakeets, tanagers, jays?

ALAN: No matter, all those. Once I went out with some boys to catch birds and I got a parrot. The way you catch a bird is you put this glue on a stick, you put nice fruit on the stick too, pineapple or banana, then you wait and that bird will land on the stick to get the fruit and then it can't fly off again.

GIRL: Euu! Papa, that's awful.

ALAN: Don't be so squeamish. Remember my parrot, Ma? It was beautiful, but it got sick and died. Parrots pair for life. So it was lonely. It died from loneliness.

GIRL: There are four thousand species of song birds . . . they have a syrinx, that's what they call the voice box of a bird, a syrinx. They have a well-developed syrinx not like other birds . . .

ALAN: That brain of yours! See, Ma, this girl is a talent. Anything she put her mind to she can do.

CHLOE: She's a gift.

ALAN: When I get a new job and when I take the pulpit from that false prophet, we will fill up the place with birds.

GIRL: Oh no, Pa. Nobody here has birds in their house.

ALAN: You don't have to follow what everybody does. You be yourself. Don't let them change you. Hear me? Besides you don't know what goes on in people's houses here. I know a man, I work with him he has a little apartment full, full of snakes. Nobody knows.

GIRL: Snakes, I don't think I like snakes. And Mother wouldn't like it. Where will we put birds anyway? It's too small here.

ALAN: Sure she will. Who wouldn't like birds. I know her better than you. Longer. She used to love birds. And you, you can take care of them. You know all about them already. You and that big brain of yours.

GIRL: I don't have to have birds, Pa, I just like to read about them.

ALAN is laughing, holding GIRL's face.

ALAN: Just like Julia. But you can have them too. You don't only have to think things, you can *do* things too.
Okay then, now next job.

GIRL: Oh do I have to go today?

ALAN: Do you have to?

ALAN stares at her sternly.

Do you have to? The Lord's work is never hard. Never hard. You hear me. They don't want me in their church. Am I discouraged? Am I discouraged?

GIRL: No. You're not discouraged.

ALAN: No. I'm not discouraged. When you do God's work the soul gets lighter and lighter, the heart is never heavy, never heavy. Repeat that after me:

GIRL/ALAN: (*together*) When you do God's work the soul gets lighter and lighter, the heart is never heavy, never heavy.

> ALAN *moves away, takes off and puts on his shirt and a jacket.*
> GIRL *turns to* CHLOE *pleadingly.*

CHLOE: Here, let me fix your hair. Nice, nice now. And you remember eh? Your Papa needs your help. Like we used to when we were home, okay?

GIRL: Yes, Mama Chloe.

CHLOE: Remember, you used to be his little soldier. Remember? You go with him and see to him. See he's . . . when he gets the passion . . .

GIRL: . . . All right. But can't you go this time, Mama Chloe?

CHLOE: Well I would yes, but you know the place better than me, don't you? You're a gifted girl, you know everything. Different here. People might trouble him. He has a gift like you, a big brain. You mind him. When he looks tired, you tell him to come home, okay?

GIRL: But Mama Chloe, I have to finish . . .

CHLOE: Finish when you get back. Your mother's working late today. You'll be back and done by the time she gets home. Don't worry. There, you're ready now.

In his jacket, ALAN picks up the Bible.

ALAN: Ready, Girl?

GIRL reluctantly follows him out.

Light fades slowly.

D-LISHUS
INNA DI WARDROBE

d-lishus is a seasoned activist and emerging artist. Her work is meant to enliven the Canadian socio-cultural landscape by injecting narratives that centre the lives and experiences of queer black women. d-lishus vivifies the multi-culti mosaic with Jamaican one-love; embodying performative afro-diasporic legacies to underscore our common humanity. Nuff respek!

Inna di Wardrobe is about what transpires when a Jamaican-Canadian woman comes out to her family by bringing her lesbian lover home for a holiday feast. As the food hits the fan, we find out that there's more to this immigrant family than meets the eye. Sometimes funny, sometimes tragic, this story pits intergenerational family dynamics and shifting social mores against the skeletons inna di wardrobe.

Inna di Wardrobe was first workshopped in May 2008 at b current's rock.paper.sistahz development series, generously supported by the Ontario Arts Council's Recommender Grants for Theatre Creators. The play was also workshopped by the frank theatre company as part of Vancouver's Queer Arts Festival in 2010 and 2013.

PLAYWRIGHT'S NOTE: A WORD ON LANGUAGE

This play is written in a fluid combination of English and Jamaican Patois. The meaning of the words is in the *sound* of them. If, when first perusing the script, the meaning seems obscure, it may be helpful to read the words aloud. Put them in your mouth and the meaning will become clear to your ears. It is completely accessible to English speakers.

The dialogue is to be crisply delivered, with fine attention to phrase constructions. The characters play against each other in rapid-fire sequence. Where the slash symbol (/) is used in a character's line, the next character to speak should begin their next line during the first character's speech, at the point indicated by the slash. If this script is delivered too slowly, it will die. If it sounds stilted/artificial, speed it up, and run it again.

If/when using actors for whom the Jamaican accent is a challenge, attention must be paid to cadence and rhythm of speech—this will contribute to making it sound like they have an accent, and lend to the overall authenticity of the piece.

* * *

Enter POPS and DAWN carrying foodstuffs for the table. GLORIA is prepping also. They begin to set up the feast. Enter CELESTE and JULES. Ad lib appropriate family banter. GHOST is seated in an extra chair at the table.

GLORIA: Okay, who want to carve di turkey?

There is a collective groan.

POPS: Awright, I will do it since nobody else don' want di honour.

GLORIA: Tanks, Pops.

DAWN: Anybody want some wine? Jules? White or red?

JULES: I'll have whatever Cee-cee's having. I'm not much of a drinker.

CELESTE: The lightest drunk you ever saw.

DAWN: *(teasing)* Okay, Cee-cee.

DAWN pours for everyone who wants wine.

POPS: Where yuh fin' dis bud, Gloria? Yuh sure yuh buy di right kin' a fowl? A never see a turkey so small.

GLORIA: Well, it was just a small group a we . . .

DAWN begins to pour herself a glass. GLORIA intercepts and takes the wine bottle.

JULES: I thought you said to expect a big family gathering.

CELESTE: Yeah, everybody usually comes over here for Big Food Day cause Mom's a killer cook.

JULES: I can tell. Everything looks really delicious, Mrs. Chambers. Thanks so much for inviting me.

GLORIA: *(continuing from above)* So A just decided not to bodda put myself through all that unnecessary trouble.

CELESTE: Where is everybody, Mom? Auntie Claire cooking today, too?

GLORIA: Well, ah—

POPS: A think Claire said she had to work for the holidays. Understaff.

CELESTE: Then what about Marcia? And Uncle Lennox and his wife?

DAWN: Marcia gone home to show off her new white fiancé.

CELESTE: Honestly? That makes, what? Number three?

POPS: Wid a baby an a bruise from each one.

DAWN: You'd think by now she would have gone back to dating brothers.

GLORIA makes a loud harrumph and pointedly looks at CELESTE.

GLORIA: She not the only one around here who should tek dat advice.

JULES: What about all your other relatives?

POPS: Maybe dem not in a holiday mood.

GLORIA: Is jus as well. What we serving up here today would turn anybody stomach.

CELESTE: / Mom!

DAWN: (*overlapping with CELESTE*) Mom!

GLORIA: What?

DAWN: That's not okay.

GLORIA: And dis is what? Perfectly appropriate?

CELESTE: Well at least it's not rude and offensive!

GLORIA: Dat's a matter of opinion.

POPS: My opinion is dat dis turkey look very dry. / Gloria, yuh bring di cranberry sauce from inna di kitchen dere?

GLORIA: Eh-eh!

She waits for POPS *to finish.*

Since when you eat cranberry sauce?

POPS: Since A reach foreign an' realize dat people do tings different over here.

GLORIA: Well you won' find any cranberry sauce in dis Jamaican household.

POPS: A buy a can weh-day.* We not in Jamaica anymore, Gloria.

GLORIA: So dat mean we must trow away everything dat we know? The bird is perfectly fine just the way it is.

CELESTE: But I'm not?

GLORIA: This is not about you.

---

* The other day.

DAWN: Well it sure isn't about the turkey.

POPS: But di cranberry sauce would still be nice.

GLORIA: There is no reason to change the way we do things just because we living in Canada now.

POPS: Gloria, yuh right. Dawn, help mi trow away dis fowl. Celeste, mek you and Julia run go Maas John house fi some goat.

GLORIA: Well fine. Since you all want to act like foreigner, A will go fi di blinking cranberry sauce.

GLORIA exits.

CELESTE: It doesn't even feel like Big Food Day with just us.

POPS: Don' worry, mi dear. Maybe everybody can meet yuh friend nex year.

CELESTE: Right! At Dawn's wedding!

JULES: Congratulations. I hear you've picked a date.

DAWN: Well . . .

POPS: What yuh keepin' it secret for? Give us the news.

Lights dim on dining table. JULES and POPS remain in suspension.

MISHKA LAVIGNE
ALBUMEN

Mishka Lavigne is a playwright and theatre translator based in Ottawa-Gatineau. She has written *Cinéma*, *Vigile*, and *Havre*. *Havre* has been translated into English (*Haven*) and German (*Hafen*), and recently won the Governor General's Literary Award for Drama. More recently, Mishka's play *Copeaux*, a movement-based theatre piece with director Éric Perron, was produced in Ottawa. *Albumen* is her first English-language play. Mishka is currently working on her new play *Shorelines*, and on her first libretto. Mishka also dabbles in writing for radio and podcasts. Mishka translates drama and literature into both French and English and is part of the Anglophone reading committee of La Maison Antoine-Vitez, an international centre for theatre translation in Paris. She is a member of the Centre des auteurs dramatiques (CEAD), the Playwrights Guild of Canada (PGC), and Playwrights' Workshop Montréal (PWM). She is a founding member of the Ottawa-based writing collective Les Poids Plumes (2013 to 2018) and also works with the Crisseurs de Feu Anonymes collective.

Albumen is a three-character play that focuses on happiness: the perception we have of the happiness of others and the steps to find happiness when we realize we are not happy with our lives. Jessa, a woman in her early thirties, decides to leave her artistic career behind but still poses for one of her art school teachers, Danielle, a photographer and very well-known artist. Jessa meets Lucas, a nurse at the blood bank where she frequently donates blood as a way to feel useful, and they begin a, mostly sexual, relationship that forces Jessa to acknowledge her own unhappiness and take steps to put herself first and change her life.

Albumen was first produced as part of the TACTICS Mainstage Series at the Arts Court Theatre, Ottawa from March 14 to 23, 2019.

* * *

JESSA and LUCAS walk in. DANIELLE greets them. Kisses, hugs, handshakes, etc.

LUCAS holds out a bottle of wine.

LUCAS: Hi! I brought you some wine. It's really nice to meet you, Danielle. I've heard so much about you from Jessa.

DANIELLE: Good things, I hope.

LUCAS: Great things. It's an honour. Jessa told me she poses for you sometimes and I've been reading up on you, looking at your work, listening to some of your interviews. Your stuff is amazing. It's so different and—I'm sorry. I don't want to seem star-struck. I'm just . . . really happy to finally meet you. It feels a little surreal to be invited to dinner at your place.

DANIELLE: Why is that?

LUCAS: I don't know . . . you're someone everyone talks about.

DANIELLE: Everyone?

LUCAS: The papers, the Internet. People talk about you, about your work. You're a celebrity.

DANIELLE: Am I?

JESSA: I think you know that you are.

Beat.

DANIELLE: Well Lucas, you may know too much about me and here I am: not knowing anything about you. We'll have to remedy the situation.

LUCAS: How about some wine before the interrogation? Do you need any help in the kitchen, Danielle?

DANIELLE: I'll get glasses. And no, you stay right here. I made lasagna. Just waiting for the oven.

She exits.

LUCAS: (*to JESSA*) I'm still really nervous. Do I look nervous?

JESSA: Calm down. Relax.

LUCAS: What's with you?

JESSA: Nothing.

LUCAS: Come on. I've asked you a million times about her. Now she invites us to dinner, which is a good thing, and you're sulking.

JESSA: I'm not.

LUCAS: You are. We've been together for weeks now and she's the first friend of yours I get to meet and it's only because she's the one who extended the invitation.

JESSA: Friend of mine?

LUCAS: I just want this to go well, okay?

DANIELLE returns with wine glasses.

DANIELLE: So, Lucas . . . Jessa tells me you're a nurse.

LUCAS: Yes. Mostly at community health centres, youth centres, free clinics. It's a great vibe. I did most of my training in the ICU at General but I just didn't feel it. I love the health centre, giving back to the community. I work in the same neighbourhood where I live. I know the people who come in, the volunteers. It's great.

DANIELLE: And you two met at a blood drive?

LUCAS: Yes. I run the blood bank at the health centre once a week. Jessa comes by often, actually. She's one of our regulars. Whole blood every fifty-six days, like clockwork. And platelet donations in between.

DANIELLE: Well, Jessa is very giving. Sounds like a great place to work.

LUCAS: It is. You get to meet a lot of different people. Talk to them. They're stuck there donating blood, they like to chat.

JESSA: You're the only nurse who talks with blood donors.

LUCAS: Well, I'm a people person. That's why I became a nurse.

(*joking to* DANIELLE) That and, you know: needles.

> DANIELLE *and* LUCAS *laugh.* JESSA *doesn't. The oven timer goes off.* DANIELLE *stands.*

No, no, let me. I insist.

> DANIELLE *smiles and sits back down.*

DANIELLE: Oven mitts are by the sink.

LUCAS: One lasagna coming right up, ladies.

> *He exits.* DANIELLE *stares at* JESSA *for a long moment.*

DANIELLE: So. This is Lucas.

JESSA: He's nice. He's a great person. We're getting along.

DANIELLE: He's in love with you.

JESSA: He's not.

DANIELLE: Whatever you say, Jessa.

> *Beat.*

Interesting choice.

JESSA: Is that the reason you invited the two of us to dinner? You wanted to see him for yourself? I've known you for ten years; you've never invited me to dinner. You never invite any of your models to dinner.

DANIELLE: I don't?

JESSA: You only invite other artists.

DANIELLE: Maybe you're not the one I invited to dinner.

JESSA doesn't answer. DANIELLE heads to the kitchen and leaves JESSA by herself. LUCAS returns.

LUCAS: (*to JESSA, concerned*) Hey. Danielle says you're not feeling well. Do you want to go?

JESSA: Danielle says—

She sees DANIELLE standing near the kitchen.

DANIELLE: (*sweetly*) It's no trouble at all. I can just freeze the lasagna. And we'll reschedule. Soon.

JESSA: (*confused*) Yes. We should go.

LUCAS: Okay. I'll drive you home. Do you want me to bring the car closer?

JESSA: No, I'm okay.

LUCAS: Are you sure?

DANIELLE: You're very compassionate, Lucas. I'm convinced you're a great nurse.

LUCAS: You should come by the clinic. Make a blood donation. We can always use more donors.

DANIELLE: Very soon. I promise.

JESSA: Let's go, Lucas.

They go to exit.

DANIELLE: I hope you feel better soon, Jessa. Don't worry about a thing. No worries.

JESSA: (*still confused*) I'm sorry.

LUCAS: (*to DANIELLE*) Make sure to drink the wine. It's a good one.

LUCAS and JESSA leave. DANIELLE takes the bottle of wine, leaves.

SUVENDRINI LENA
THE ENCHANTED LOOM

Suvendrini Lena is a playwright and neurologist. She lives and works in Toronto. Her first play, *The Enchanted Loom* was co-produced by Cahoots Theatre and Factory Theatre in 2016. She is currently an artist in residence at The Theatre Centre and Cahoots. In addition to clinical work in neuropsychiatry and neurology she integrates theatrical practice into her role as a clinical teacher of medical students and residents.

The Sri Lankan civil war has left many scars on Thangan and his family, most noticeably the loss of his eldest son and crippling epileptic seizures brought on by his torture during the war. As the final days of the war play out, the family watches from Toronto, where a neurological procedure provides them with a chance to heal. This poetic play, part medical, part mystical is a harrowing tale of loss and hope that reminds us of the joys and pain of unconditional love for family, and freedom.

The Enchanted Loom was produced by Cahoots Theatre in association with Factory Theatre from November 10 to 27, 2016.

* * *

A doctor's office. MENDOZA is examining THANGAN seamlessly as she interviews him. MENDOZA could perform the neurological exam in her sleep. Her movements are dance-like and crisp, even brusque.

MENDOZA uses pure medical language throughout. It is like a secret language in which she and WAGDY are fluent and into which KANAN is being initiated. Its use alienates THANGAN, SEVI, and KAVITHA.

MENDOZA: Hello, Thangan. Sevi, Kanan . . . and you must be—

KAVITHA: Kavitha.

THANGAN: I would like to talk about the surgery.

MENDOZA: We've discussed surgery before, at length. Has something changed?

Silence.

Well, why don't you come and sit up here and we'll see.

THANGAN looks at KAVITHA.

THANGAN: Should I—

MENDOZA: Just your shoes and socks. Are you taking all your medication, every day?

SEVI: No.

KAVITHA: He thinks they make him stupid.

MENDOZA shines a light in each of his eyes.

He does forget stuff.

MENDOZA examines his eye movements.

MENDOZA: How are you sleeping?

THANGAN: The night is full of muttering, pacing, and lately some bells.

He looks at KAVITHA.

Everyone speaks, even Sevi. She speaks to me in her dreams. I listen.

KANAN: He has nocturnal seizures.

THANGAN: I have nightmares.

MENDOZA: (*to herself*) Sleep fragmentation. R.E.M. intrusions?

SEVI: He doesn't remember.

MENDOZA proceeds to examine his visual fields. He covers one eye then the other. He makes errors counting her fingers.

THANGAN: Two—one—two—three.

MENDOZA: (*to KANAN*) Watch the left upper field.

(*to SEVI*) Tell me what you see at night.

THANGAN: Two—one—two—one.

KANAN: (*to MENDOZA*) A left upper quadrantanopia from a right inferior temporal lesion.

SEVI: He cries out.

KAVITHA: For Kavalan.

SEVI: Then he reaches out—

MENDOZA: Which arm?

SEVI: Left—

KANAN: (*to MENDOZA*) And a right frontal lesion?

MENDOZA: How many seizures did you have last month? Close your eyes.

She tries to pry them open.

SEVI: One a day at dawn.

KAVITHA: At least.

KANAN: I wonder if we even recognize all the partial seizures.

MENDOZA: Smile. Shut your mouth, tight.

She tries to pry his mouth open.

Every day?

KAVITHA: Five were really bad, while he watched the news. He shakes all over and pees and sometimes I think he might not wake up.

Beat.

MENDOZA pricks him with a pin three times, in each of the three nerve sectors. He winces.

MENDOZA: How does it start? Is it always the same?

THANGAN: Usually.

She taps his jaw with a reflex hammer.

It's a surprise—a thousand butterflies fluttering up inside me—for a moment—it's pleasant. Thoughts come fast, fast, at last, I could . . . compose a poem . . . or go for a drive.

She taps his arms with a reflex hammer. His biceps reflex is more prominent on the left.

MENDOZA: (*muttered*) Left is brisk.

THANGAN: Then my wings collapse . . . I feel a coiling dread inside . . . until . . .

KANAN: (*also muttered, to MENDOZA*) Amygdala.

MENDOZA continues to check THANGAN's reflexes and tone.

Relax, Appa—

MENDOZA: Let me move your limbs. As if you are a rag doll. And the other spells?

THANGAN: Sometimes there is this long moment of perfect solitude and I behold my son's face—Kavalan's—radiant like the sun. Then it grows dark. He cries . . . He breaks into shards . . . there is pain . . . electric current applied to each of my fingers —

SEVI: Anban. *[Dear.]* You remember it.

Look at his hand. These are memories.

MENDOZA: Olfactory hallucinations?

She scratches the soles of his feet with a key.

Sorry.

(to self) Babinski left.

(to KANAN) This is new.

(to THANGAN) Do you ever smell anything odd?

THANGAN: Burnt flesh.

KANAN: *(to himself)* Uncus.

MENDOZA: So many wounds.

Beat.

SEVI: Can't you do something?

MENDOZA: Put your socks and shoes on. Can you walk like this, heel to toe?

THANGAN sways as if he is drunk. KAVITHA gets up and starts practising the heel-to-toe walk, doing it quickly backwards and forwards.

It's the medication.

THANGAN: Can you help me?

MENDOZA: Did you go to see the psychiatrist I recommended?

THANGAN: Yes. He was a very kind man. He offered me more drugs. He offered to talk to me about my "recurrent traumatic memories." He thinks I am crazy. She (*SEVI*) thinks I am a ghost. What do you think?

KAVITHA: Appa is not crazy.

MENDOZA: It's complicated. The injury you sustained in prison has left scars in your brain. Each scar causes a different type of seizure.

She picks up a model of the brain and points out different regions as she speaks.

An insular seizure can cause pain, an uncal seizure the smell of fire. A seizure in the frontal motor cortex makes your hand shake. Even the fear—inferior temporal lobe seizures cause pure, visceral, fear, and can trigger paranoia, even psychosis. The number of scars makes it—

THANGAN: And Kavalan's face?

MENDOZA: All visions aren't seizures . . . You are haunted. This is why I hoped you would work with Dr. Levitsky . . .

THANGAN: Listen. Please. Each night I dream I'm on a stony beach. With a necklace. It falls. Shatters—beads scatter. I grasp for them. But it's too late . . . some are lost to the sea forever. Each time I seize, more are lost forever.

MENDOZA: I know.

THANGAN: No you don't—

SEVI: Doctor. If you take part of him out, out of his brain, you can give *him* back to us?

MENDOZA: The truth is I don't know. Epilepsy changes a person; the surgery can change a person.

KANAN: We need change.

MENDOZA: It may not be safe.

THANGAN: What have I got to lose?

MENDOZA: All right, all right. I'll admit you to the monitoring unit. We need better electrophysiological evidence.

They rise to exit.

KAVITHA: (*whispers*) Appa, you're not crazy.

THANGAN: Why do you say that, Kavi?

KAVITHA: Kavalan talks to me too.

ROB SALERNO
RAW

Rob Salerno is a playwright, actor, and producer. Rob founded Ten Foot Pole Theatre, the home for his original plays, *Balls*, *Fucking Stephen Harper*, *Big in Germany*, *First Day Back*, and *Palau*, which have been produced in cities across Canada, the United States, and overseas. *First Day Back* was nominated for two Dora Mavor Moore Awards for writing and performance. He wrote for the *2017 CBS Diversity Sketch Comedy Showcase* and from 2017 to 2019 was head writer of the monthly sketch comedy show *Mike Pence's Big Queer Nightmare*. Rob holds an Honours B.A. from McGill University and an M.A. in Drama from University of Toronto. He is a graduate of the Upright Citizens Brigade Los Angeles Sketch Writing and Improv programs, and has studied performance with the Groundlings and Playhouse West. Reach him on Twitter/Instagram/YouTube @robsalerno.

Stephen and James become bound by sex, violence, and desire after a sexual encounter where Stephen doesn't tell James that he is HIV-positive. As their relationship evolves, through lust, anger, desire, and back, they struggle to find a way to live with each other and themselves. Complicating this is Dax, a sex-positive graduate student who challenges their prejudices and hypocrisies.

Scenes from *RAW* were first workshopped by Ten Foot Pole Theatre at the Toronto Fringe Festival from July 3 to 15, 2012. A reading of *RAW* was produced at the 2015 International Dublin Gay Theatre Festival.

* * *

There's a knock at the door.

The knocking gets louder and lights come up revealing a filthy bachelor walk-up apartment. DAX is in his boxers and a dirty undershirt, rolling a joint.

DAX: Jeezes, calm down I'm coming.

DAX opens the door to see JAMES and STEPHEN there.

DAX: Oh hey, Pampers.

STEPHEN: Pampers?

JAMES: Don't ask. Hi, Dax, sorry to come unannounced. This is my friend, Stephen. I think you've met.

DAX: Stephen . . . doesn't ring a bell, dude.

JAMES: We, uh, wanted to talk to you . . . do you have a minute?

DAX nods them in. They enter the apartment. JAMES finds a place to sit. STEPHEN stays standing, near the door.

DAX: What do you want?

JAMES: Well, Stephen was scrolling through my chat history and he saw your picture and—

DAX: Got jealous?

STEPHEN: Jesus, no! We've fucked.

DAX: You've fucked?

JAMES: No, I mean, yes, but no, he thinks you two have fucked.

DAX: We fucked?

STEPHEN: We've fucked.

JAMES: Apparently, you've fucked.

DAX: Fuck. Well, Dax's first law of homodynamics—within a closed system all faggots will eventually fuck.

JAMES: Is that the "conservation of sodomy" principle?

DAX: So? You want a threeway or something? 'Cause, look, thing is, Pampers, James, you're fun an' all, but money's a little tight this month, so I'm really only having sex now with guys who'll pay me for it, I gotta stick to that.

JAMES: What?

STEPHEN: Are you, you fucking kidding me?

DAX's phone gets a text message, and he starts typing out a response.

DAX: Hey, man, nothing personal. Just trade, bro. If I give it away for free it's not worth anything, right? But maybe if you'd be down to video it for my thesis research . . .

STEPHEN: You're a fucking whore.

JAMES: Stephen, it's not worth it.

DAX: James, I'm worth it.

STEPHEN: You have AIDS! And you're whoring?!

DAX: I'm HIV-positive. So? I guess you both are, too. And I'm only a situational sex worker. I'm actually a sexual autoethnographer.

JAMES: You said that before, and I'm actually not sure what that means.

DAX: Autoethnography is a kind of research where the author uses self-reflection to explore personal experience and connect his autobiographical story to wider cultural and social meanings. It's all the rage in sociology and queer studies.

STEPHEN: They give Ph.D.s in being Carrie Bradshaw?

DAX: Who the fuck is Carrie Bradshaw?

JAMES: One of the old ladies from the *Sex and the City* movies.

DAX: Oh, yeah, my department is really excited about my thesis research.

STEPHEN: Which is just . . . fucking guys and writing about it?

DAX: That's a little reductive, but . . .

STEPHEN: You don't care that you could give it to other guys?

DAX: Whatever dude, I use a condom if they want and I take my pills.

STEPHEN: But you're just— How long have you been poz?

DAX gets another text, which he responds to.

DAX: Ugh. I dunno. Who ever knows anything, bro?

STEPHEN: What the hell does that mean?

DAX: Maybe I always had it. Maybe everyone has it. Or maybe every-one should have it. Homos. I mean, isn't the erotic thing about being queer the risk, the danger, the dirt? The shame? We used to have to hookup in toilets and dark alleys. We could've been busted by the cops at any minute. We used to have to hide our sex, but now it's neutered and used to sell fucking bank accounts and McDoubles. The government gives us money for parades and if the mayor doesn't show up and clap for us, everyone's pissed at *him*. And now we can't even let queer teens be bullied anymore. How fucking *gay*. You think it's better for kids not to get a little rush of danger when they ogle the football captain? I tell ya, that's not preparing kids for any kinda life. Any interesting life at least.

STEPHEN: Well, I didn't have it when we—

DAX: So we fucked, eh? At Steamworks or a party?

STEPHEN: How long have you been poz?

DAX: . . . It's been a few years. So what?

STEPHEN: Are you retarded? Do you even know what AIDS is?

DAX: Hey, fuck you. You come in my house, think you can insult me?

JAMES: Why don't we all just calm down here. Stephen didn't mean—

STEPHEN: The fuck I didn't!

DAX: How do you even know this fucker?

JAMES: He, uh, gave me the HIV.

DAX: . . . *The* HIV?

JAMES: It's grammatical.

DAX: So this is the guy, eh? I see what you were saying before. Still, kinda awesome you know your guy. Wish I knew which guy gave it to me.

STEPHEN: What?

DAX: I wanted it so bad, bro. I didn't know jack shit when I came out. Just this fuckin' sixteen-year-old runaway from fucking Granby, Ontario, bet you never even heard of it, doesn't even come up on Google Maps. Over there, no one gave a shit about me. And there was nothing to do. And I came to Toronto, and no one gave a shit about me here either. But there's shit to do here, man. I fucking changed everything about me. All the shit I was scared of before. Everything I did to fit in that narrow space between fitting in with all the other kids and being just different enough to stand out without getting killed. Cut off all my hair, got tats, even changed my name. You know Dax ain't even my real name?

STEPHEN / JAMES: (*mocking/deadpan*) No. / Really?

DAX: Yeah! Still no one cares. I go to the bars, pick up, fuck, get fucked . . . It wasn't bein' gay holding me back. There's a fucking million gay people in Toronto—

STEPHEN: Not—

JAMES: Don't—

DAX: Gay, here in the city? That's just the same bullshit everywhere else in society. Same cliques, same jobs, same obsessions with order and cleanliness and fitting in. More money, sure, flashier clothes. But it's still all bullshit.

One time I hear these uptight queens talking about a "digusting" jock strap party happening at the Eagle, and I'm like, "If that's where these guys aren't gonna be, that's where I wanna be." And I go, and it's just . . . this is my tribe, man. And the fuckin' parties, shit regular people got no idea about. Fuckin' dozens of dudes piled on each other, fucking, sucking, sweaty, swinging from the rafters fucking. And no one's scared. And everyone loves everyone and takes everyone and gives and shares, man. You'd've seen if you hadn't bailed on that party, Pampers. Everyone wants you there, right? 'Cause we're rare. Makes you special.

JAMES: But what about your health, your life, how can you have just traded that away for, for what, some sex?

DAX: Don't talk about my health. I'm not sick. Infected but not sick. I'm, what, future sick? We're all future sick someday. Seriously, who came up with the moral imperative to be healthy all the time?

JAMES: I'm not moralizing! I'm . . . concerned, like anyone would be, when you see someone doing something risky.

DAX: Pfft. Are you this concerned when you see someone riding a bike without a helmet? A helmet's just a condom for your head. In other words: my body, my choice.

Man, you still think HIV's gotta be some sad story. My story's awesome. I fucking loved this crew of guys I was rolling with. We used to all meet up at this house in Cabbagetown, and it'd be all night long, just different guys fucking me, fifteen, twenty, I'd lose count. And I'd fucking take it all, like a fucking champ. When I finally got the bug, it was like I was tattooed on my inside, like I'm part of this brotherhood. I'm part of something bigger than me now. Being poz, it's like the ultimate expression of who I am, who we are.

STEPHEN: Not everyone chooses this.

DAX: Oh, did you get HIV from a blood transfusion in the '80s? No? Mic drop.

STEPHEN: You gave it to me.

DAX puts down the phone and goes to hug STEPHEN. STEPHEN accepts the embrace. It's a surprising moment of relief. A burden lifted.

DAX: . . . You're welcome.

STEPHEN: You son of a bitch!

STEPHEN pushes DAX away, and goes to hit him, but JAMES holds him back.

DAX: I think I do remember you now. Steamworks, right? You made me put on a dome, but it broke. Is that scar new? It's badass, dude.

STEPHEN: Why didn't you tell me—?

DAX: Whatever bro, you were in Steamworks. I know guys who got it just by walking around in there without flip flops.

JAMES: Now that can't be true. Wait, can it?

DAX: Who knows, right? I had to take like a thousand loads before I got it.

STEPHEN: You know what you've cost me? I lost my job. I'm gonna lose my house. I might even lose my freedom.

JAMES: Those things aren't really Dax's fault.

DAX: You guys with your terrified moralizing and your high horses. You don't even see that this is our culture.

STEPHEN: Excuse me?

DAX: We belong to a culture that includes Freddie Mercury and Rock Hudson and Keith Haring. Just like my cum got into you and through you into him, we could trace it all back and see there's a little Liberace in all of us. That's our people. That's our history. Guys like that made music and art and led a sexual revolution that changed the world. You poor fucks don't get that your lives didn't end when you got HIV— they fucking began. Both of you, so ashamed of your own sex that you've got to stamp out my "immorality" just to validate your own hypocrisy. The only way we're ever going to have real pride, is when we embrace our complete perversion, obliterating every last vestige of shame, and fear, and self-doubt so we can own who we are. I know who I am. I'm a filthy pig and I love it. Who are you?

JAMES: Is that from something?

DAX: Look, you guys are pretty cool, so tell you what, you wanna hook up still, I can do it like I'm just charging one of you. Two for the price of one. Two hundred for an hour.

I remember you've got a tight little hole. I can loosen it up for you.

DAX makes an obscene gesture with his tongue to STEPHEN.

JAMES gives DAX a scolding look.

One-fifty?

STEPHEN: How can you not give a damn about people you've hurt?

DAX: Hurt you? I gave you what you wanted: a hot fuck from a young stud. I got a dangerous look and you get off on that. Let me guess, you're some hot-shit businessy type. Rich. Grew up in the city, too, I bet. You think you're real sophisticated. You took one look at me and thought "trash." Stupid, hopeless nothing but he's got a big dick. And you get off on that, too, thinkin' you're better'n me.

JAMES: Well he read you pretty quick.

STEPHEN: Oh shut up.

JAMES: Hey!

DAX: You're just an anecdote in a chapter of my thesis. "Anonymous Sex Among the Closeted Upper Crust."

JAMES: Groundbreaking.

DAX: And maybe you are better'n me. But us fucking? That was a transaction, man. But this new deal I'm offering? It's time-limited. So what's it going to be?

DAX takes off his shirt and approaches STEPHEN. STEPHEN snaps, punches DAX in the face, then tackles him to the ground, and continues beating him.

STEPHEN: You disgusting goddamn piece of shit whore.

JAMES tries to separate them.

JAMES: Hey! Get off him!

STEPHEN shoves JAMES off him, and he reels back to the ground.

STEPHEN: Fuck you!

JAMES: Fuck you!

STEPHEN, who is now straddling DAX on the ground, suddenly notices:

STEPHEN: Fuck, are you hard?!

STEPHEN gets off DAX, and DAX half sits up. DAX is bleeding from his mouth.

DAX: That's right. I am. I'm a disgusting goddamn piece of shit whore. And what does that make you? That you let me fuck you and begged me for it? That right now you can't help but think about bending me over that couch and teaching me all about responsibility?

STEPHEN: Can you believe this?

JAMES: Actually, I want to know too. What does that make you?

STEPHEN: Are you taking his side?

JAMES: What are we doing here, Stephen? Did we just come here so you could feel better about yourself, looking down from your "moral high ground" on some loser—

DAX: Hey!

JAMES: —sorry—that you can blame for all your problems? 'Cause that's not what I signed up for.

STEPHEN: Screw both of you.

STEPHEN exits.

DAX gets up, wipes his mouth off on his shirt.

JAMES: Shit. He was my ride.

DAX: No worries, bro. I liked your dick, man. Now that we're alone . . . hundred bucks'll get you an hour.

JAMES: No offence, man, but do I look like the sort of guy who needs to pay for sex?

DAX: Needs to? Nah. No one really needs to, bro. But wants to? I think you want to. Come on. Eighty for just mouth stuff. How much you got?

DAX licks JAMES's neck and JAMES is caught up in DAX's seduction. Goes to grab his wallet, and remembers that he doesn't have it.

JAMES: Shit! I left my wallet at Stephen's. Um. I don't suppose you could lend me bus fare?

DAX: That's not really how this works, bro.

Lights fade out.

PAST

LEONARD LINKLATER
JUSTICE

Leonard Linklater is a founding co-artistic director of Gwaandak Theatre, as well as a playwright and journalist for CBC. He was born and raised in Inuvik, Northwest Territories, and is a member of the Vuntut Gwitchin First Nation. His first play *Sixty Below* received seven Dora nominations for its 1997 Toronto production with Native Earth Performing Arts, including for best script, and with his wife Patti Flather is the inaugural recipient of the Borealis Prize: The Commissioner of Yukon Award for Literary Contribution. Since 2000, Leonard has co-produced various Gwaandak productions. He is a member of the Playwrights Guild of Canada.

You must ask yourself if justice has been served when a young man out to seek fortune during the Klondike Gold Rush is gunned down in a misunderstanding—in a meeting of cultures during a hectic time. Is justice served by the law that is brought in and imposed on the land and the original people? Linklater examines the gold rush era case of the Nantuck brothers, where living up to clan obligations lands them in a new justice system at a time when law and order is in demand.

Justice was co-produced by Gwaandak Theatre and the National Arts Centre in Whitehorse, Yukon, and Ottawa, Ontario, in September 2012 and May 2013.

* * *

Prospectors' camp.

FRANK: Pay.

Beat.

You.

Beat.

You pay.

FOX: Huh? Pay for what?

FRANK: You pay.

FOX: What are you saying? We pay for what?

FRANK: Family.

FOX: We don't have family here. Billy? I told you we can't trust Indians.

FRANK: Family. Dead. Yesterday. Years . . .

MEEHAN: Maybe he's talking about the land of his people, that we have to pay for passage or use of the land or something like that.

FOX: I've never heard of such a thing. Billy, what do you make of this? I mean everywhere I've been so far, seems there's no restrictions.

MEEHAN: I can't say what their rules are. In Juneau no one was demanding any payment and there's all kinds of logging, fishing and mining going on.

FOX: As far as I know the only time you pay is when you stake a claim. And that goes to the government. The only Indians to ask for money is those packing supplies over the pass. Other than that I don't ever remember any Indians asking us for payment.

MEEHAN: What do we owe?

MEEHAN stares blankly.

Pay? What?

MEEHAN motions to the supplies.

FOX: What are you doing? Tell him we paid at the pass.

FRANK: Two people.

MEEHAN: Yes, yes. We are two people. What do we pay?

FRANK looks around, clearly not prepared for this.

FRANK: Flour?

MEEHAN: Yeah, there's some there. Take what you need.

FOX: Hey, we can't be giving them all our provisions.

MEEHAN: We've got enough here to last us a year. The hungriest Indians in the world couldn't eat that much.

FRANK: How long stay?

FRANK motions, gesturing around.

MEEHAN: Only as long as it takes to make a fortune in the Klondike. We understand that a man can make a good living. Have you any news on what is happening?

FRANK: Lots White man go that way. No come back.

FOX: It's a long way.

FRANK: That way. No good.

MEEHAN: Many of my people believe there is good down river. At least better than what they have at home.

FRANK: Nothing good down north.

FRANK examines a pot.

FOX: There's supposed to be lots of gold.

MEEHAN: What's wrong with down, I mean, up north?

FRANK: No good. Bad. Bad spirits. Danger.

MEEHAN: How do you mean danger?

FRANK: People no come back.

FOX: What's he trying to say Billy?

MEEHAN: Probably just talking about the rapids.

(to FRANK) We know about the rapids. The riffles. Fast water. We know there's places to watch for, but we think we'll be all right.

FRANK: Flour. Bread.

MEEHAN: You're going to need some baking powder. It's in that tin over there. Help yourself.

FRANK: This?

FOX / MEEHAN: No.

FOX: You don't want that one. That's arsenic.

FRANK: Ass-nick? Bread?

MEEHAN: No. Not bread. This is for the vermin. For little animals. Trapping. It's poison.

FRANK: Poy—sinn?

MEEHAN: It's poison.

MEEHAN makes a choking motion.

Danger. If you eat . . . it could kill you.

(*motioning*) You want the other tin.

FRANK realizes this is the same/similar substance that killed his clan members. Drops the can and leaves hurriedly with a pot and flour.

* * *

Court room.

MCGUIRE: Order!!

MCGUIRE pounds the gavel three times, deliberate and distinct.

Order in the court! I call this court to order.

The crowd noises fade.

This, the Supreme Court of the Yukon Territory, is now set to hear the matter of Regina versus Jim Nantuck and Frank Nantuck. The Nantucks are charged with the murder of William Meehan on or about the tenth day of May, 1898.

Much mumbling and harrumphing from the crowd.

It is alleged the accused did shoot to death William Meehan as Mr. Meehan and his prospecting partner, Christian Fox, were embarking on a boat trip along the McClintock River that fateful morning.

Beat.

Defence counsel. How do your clients plead?

LISLE: That is a difficult question to answer your honour, my clients do not deny they shot and killed Mr. Meehan, and wounded Mr. Fox.

The crowd jeers and shouts.

MCGUIRE: Order! This may be a drinking establishment by night. And you may be accustomed to a little boisterous behaviour. But right now this is my courtroom! And I will have order in my court. Is that clear?

Beat.

You may proceed, Mr. Lisle.

LISLE: Your honour, my clients only have a rudimentary knowledge of English. Their first language is Tagish, I believe it is an inland dialect of Tlingit, a very complex language of the coast. This court is situated some three hundred miles north of their homeland. We do not have people here who speak that language. We've employed an interpreter who knows a trade dialect. Whether it is sufficient to explain the seriousness of the charges is quite impossible to say.

MCGUIRE: So, have they indicated how they want to plead?

LISLE: I'm not sure we've done all that we could, Your Honour. Without interpreters who are fluent in the language, we can not go beyond a superficial knowledge of what they are trying to tell us. Certainly they do not deny their part in the shooting.

The crowd jeers, harrumphs.

MCGUIRE: Order!

Beat.

So, you admit to killing Mr. Meehan?

The Nantucks nod tentatively, unconvincingly.

Uh-huh . . .

Mr. Lisle, did you explain to these men the serious nature of the charges they face?

LISLE: As best I could, Your Honour. The Indian lacks any under-standing of our justice system.

MCGUIRE: Yes. Yes. But do they understand they could be hanged for this? I want to ensure in no uncertain terms, that these men, regard-less of their ignorance, realize the gravity of the situation. Do they understand that it is murder?

LISLE: I cannot say, not knowing the word for murder in their lan-guage or even if they have one. My clients do not deny they killed Mr. Meehan. Whether they know if it was murder, homicide, or even if it was wrong is beyond me. They don't seem to think so. With the court's leave, they don't understand why both of them must hang. Indeed, it took some time for me to explain to them why they were arrested in the first place. They seem to have some notion they were collecting on a debt. I have no idea what that debt may be.

MCGUIRE: Mr. Lisle, I can not profess to be an expert in how they do things in Nova Scotia, or what they may teach at Dalhousie. This may be a new court in a new jurisdiction—

LISLE: And I understand it was set up in quite a hurry, Your Honour. I also understand there is some question as to whether it was done correctly or not. But—

MCGUIRE: *(with authority)* I will have no shenanigans in my court, Mr. Lisle. There will be no appeals based on lack of, or derogation from, procedure. I will be damned if anyone can say in hindsight that these men have not had their day in court, or that it was not fair. Mr. Lisle. Do you understand me?

LISLE: Yes, Your Honour. Much like you I want things to be fair. I've looked into their eyes and I see proud men.

The realization of what the Nantucks have been trying to com-municate creeps in to LISLE.

They are willing to take responsibility, but they have questions. There does not seem to be remorse. It's almost as if the men killed William Meehan as a last resort.

MCGUIRE: A last resort? To what? Did they fear their winter supply of food was leaving with these men?

LISLE: Again Your Honour, the interpreter's translation was not suffi-cient to explain the intricacies of their thinking.

MCGUIRE: But, if I understand you Mr. Lisle, they do not deny killing William Meehan?

LISLE: No, Your Honour.

MCGUIRE: Now that you've taken us around this delightful little jour-ney, how do your clients plead?

JIM / FRANK: *(mutters)* Not guilty.

LISLE: Not guilty, Your Honour.

MCGUIRE: Very good Mr. Lisle. Not guilty pleas will be entered for Jim Nantuck and Frank Nantuck.

MCGUIRE strikes the gavel.

RENELTTA ARLUK
PAWÂKAN ᒪᕀᑯᕁᕹᕽᐧ

Reneltta Arluk is an Inuvialuit, Cree, and Dene woman from the Northwest Territories. She is a graduate of the B.F.A. Acting program from the University of Alberta and founder of Akpik Theatre, a professional, northern-focused Indigenous theatre company. Reneltta authored *Thoughts and Other Human Tendencies* with BookLand Press, which is available in English, French, and Cree. She has been published in *Inuit Quarterly, Arc Poetry Magazine, Where Is The Hope: An Anthology Of Short Climate Change Plays*, and has contributed to the Indigenous Performing Arts Alliance. Reneltta's plays include *TUMIT*, a radio adaptation of *I Count Myself Among Them* by Richard Van Camp, and is currently working on a play about Tookoolito, an Inuk woman guide to Charles Francis Hall in the late 1800s.

A groundbreaking takeover of Shakespeare's darkest play into Cree history, legend, and cosmology, *Pawâkan ᒪᕀᑯᕁᕹᕽ*is set before the creation of Treaty 6 territory, when Plains Cree were allied with Stoney Nakoda and were at war with Blackfoot over territory, food, supplies, and trade. This was a time when true autonomy existed among Indigenous peoples, allowing for the abundance of their spirits, their wisdom, practices, makers, tricksters, shifters—their darkness and light. This was a time when the Canadian government was making their way west with Sir John A. MacDonald as its leader. The harsh environments bring immense fear, starvation, and uncertainty together and awaken the darkest of Cree spirits, the Wihtiko—a cannibalistic being with insatiable greed.

Pawâkan Lᒋᑯᕋᐦᑊ is a full-length play commissioned by the Stratford Festival, and is still in development. The play is inspired by working with the youth of Frog Lake First Nation, and shared stories from Elders in the Treaty 6 region. The original development of concept was with Owen Morris and students from Chief Napeweaw School. Some stories originate from the Frog Lake, Loon Lake, and Onion Lake region. Acknowledgements to Mary Ann Dillon, Rose Dillon, Henry Smith, Raymond Quinney, Cecile Dion, and Cultural Advisor Gary Berland.

* * *

Fall. Dusk. A forest.

The scarce sound of Coyotes howling from different directions. In the shadows of trees emerge the Coyote Howlers. There can be as many or as few as needed. They jump, swagger, dodge into a clearing, shape-shift into human form as scavengers.

WIYÔYÔWAK: Tanisih Etahkamikisîyin, Nitotem?
(What have you been up to, kin?)

WIYÔYÔWAK: Looking up nuns' skirts.

WIYÔYÔWAK: Kîya Maka?
(And you?)

WIYÔYÔWAK: A Chief's wife had dryfish in her lap,
And chew'd, and chew'd, and chew'd—
"Give me," I said.
"Bugger off!" the big-bummed Môswah cried.
Her husband to summer camping gone, setting nets for fish:
But as a pike I'll thither swim,
And, like a Catholic church without a hymn,
I'll do, I'll do, and I'll do.

WIYÔYÔWAK: I'll give thee a current.

WIYÔYÔWAK: Nîsta Mîna.
(And I another.)

WIYÔYÔWAK: And I, myself as a beggar, will stay with them in the lodge. I will cover his eyes with hunger and have him think his grandson a beaver. He and his grandson alone, just a little boy. He will think, "Oh, that beaver is fat and will make a good meal for me." So he will roast the baby over the fire. When the babe is well roasted, he will try him and say, "Mmm, this is pretty good." In that same summer night will return his daughter and son-in-law from hunting. His mind will clear and see what he has done. Look what I have.

WIYÔYÔWAK: Yip yip!

WIYÔYÔWAK: Here I have the husband's eye.
Wreck'd as homeward he did cry.

The Coyote Howlers howl and gather.

ALL WIYÔYÔWAK: (*sung as a forty-nine*) We will not be forgotten
Our Spirit will grow and grow
Bring winter ice and harden
Macikosisân, soul
The Wihtiko
Peace! Aho!

The Coyote Howlers shape-shift back into fur form, waiting.

MACIKOSISÂN and MÔSÂPEW enter.

MACIKOSISÂN: So foul and fair a day I have not seen.

WIYÔYÔWAK: Kâkisteyimiht oskinîkiw, Macikosisân.
(Worthy Young Man, Macikosisân.)

MACIKOSISÂN: Kîkwâya? You know me?
(What?)

The Coyotes, seeing a mouse, shift into Howler Beings and chase it. They are trying to stamp it with their feet. One is attempting to shoot it with a bow and arrow. The other is gnashing at it with its mouth.

MÔSÂPEW: What are these? So scraggly with their matted hair. So wild in their skins.
They look not of this land and yet are on it.
Pimâtisîyin, Ci!
(Live you? Tell me!)

WIYÔYÔWAK: Snarl!

MÔSÂPEW: You understand me but speak not Cree? You should be human but do not seem so.

The Coyote Howlers encircle MACIKOSISÂN and MÔSÂPEW. They snap at their bodies and eyes. MACIKOSISÂN and MÔSÂPEW give defence. The Coyote Howlers jump back and gather into one creature.

ALL WIYÔYÔWAK: Macikosisân, Macikosisân. Kâkisteyimiht Oskinekiw you are, and War Chief next.
By a full moon light and when day becomes night.
A greater Chief than Wîpastim you will be. Macikosisân.

A wind blows through.

WIYÔYÔWAK: Ewakôma Kâke Mekawîyin.
(This is what you have been given.)

WIYÔYÔWAK: (*referring to Cree just spoken*) Your fate is laid before you.

WIYÔYÔWAK: I just said that.

MÔSÂPEW: And, what have you to say to this warrior?
What vision have you for me?

ALL WIYÔYÔWAK: (*chuffed*) Ahh, uhm.
Your son will be Chief.
Aho!

MACIKOSISÂN: If you can look into the seeds of time and say which
will grow and which will not.
Tell it to me then. Let not modesty be your virtue now.

ALL WIYÔYÔWAK: When the snow falls your Pawâkan calls.
Yip! Yip! Arrooo!

> *The Coyote Howlers jump apart and scamper as four-leggeds
> into the forest. Gone.*

MACIKOSISÂN: Stay, you twisted-tongued creatures!
Hâw Acimoh!
(Tell me more!)
Gone.

MÔSÂPEW: Had I not seen, I would not have believed.

MACIKOSISÂN: Same here.
(*teasing*) Your son will be Chief.

MÔSÂPEW: (*teasing*) You will be War Chief.

An inhalation.

MACIKOSISÂN: (*seriously*) And Okimâw too.

Pause.

Neee.

A whistle is heard.

KÎMÔCÂPEW enters.

KÎMÔCÂPEW: Tanisi Macikosisân!

MACIKOSISÂN: Ehâ.

KÎMÔCÂPEW: Okimâw Wîpastim was pleased to hear of your latest win, Macikosisân. An Asinîyipwât ally came and told the story of your vicious slaughter against our mighty enemy, the Bloods. He was surprised to hear of the raid from Pikânawîyiniwak, but not surprised to hear you butchered every one of them. Our Chief battle-cried. He had Otepwestamâkew deliver news of your bravery to the camp, for how you once again defended our territory. We have many of their horses now and even more buffalo.

KÎMÔCÂPEW takes off a bone plate.

This gift is for you, good warrior cousin. For your fearlessness and grit, Okimâw Wîpastim had me come and name you from Kâkisteyimiht oskinikiw to War Chief, and to let you know the best stallion is yours.

KÎMÔCÂPEW offers a few gifting dance steps.

Kitatamiskâtin!
(Congratulations!)

MACIKOSISÂN: Ay Hay. I am humbled.
What do you think will become of your son now?

MÔSÂPEW: I will think no more of it, in fear of it becoming something bigger than I can face.

MACIKOSISÂN: Before I went on my fast to learn of my Pawâkan, we were suffering. Family members lost. It was cold. I was scared but I held my breath, waiting for it to come to me. I dreamt the hills around me became heads of bears. They were alive. I could feel their breath. Hot. When I woke up, I was surrounded by ice. Yes. There is always something bigger to face, Môsâpew. If chance will have me Chief, then chance can name me. That I will not fight.

MÔSÂPEW: There can be no light when dark is spoken. Trust.

KÎMÔCÂPEW: Hey, War Chief, your stallion awaits you, Kweyâho!

MACIKOSISÂN: Enough of this talk. Astam!

Exeunt.

MIKE CZUBA
REPRISE

Mike Czuba is a writer, director, story editor, and dramaturg with a B.F.A. and M.F.A. in Playwriting. Originally from Montreal, he is currently a performance instructor at the University of Calgary and co-founder of the performance collective Dancing Monkey Laboratories (dancingmonkeylab.com). His plays, including *I Am I* (Original Works Publishing) and *Satie et Cocteau: A Rehearsal of a Play of a Composer by a Poet*, have been internationally produced. A short film based on Mike's play *Humanoid—A Love Supreme* entitled *The Void* was an official selection in the 2017 Philip K. Dick Film Festival. His TYA play *Boy Sees Flying Saucer* (based on a true and original story by Brian Dorscht) was awarded the Laurie Award from The Growing Stage: The Children's Theatre of New Jersey (2018). Mike is writing a book on creative process called *No Shortcuts—this book will not hug you*.

Upon learning of his father's death, musician Steven Booker spends an agonizing and fantastical day and night trying to dismiss the man he hated so much but knew so little about. Through a series of memories and the reality of his current situation, Steven discovers that he is very much his father's son. As hard as he tries to avoid it, only by going to his father's funeral will he be able to move forward and become the man he wants to be and not the man he has become. The story is structured like a song with music used to propel and increase the power of the narrative without removing the audience from it.

Reprise received a staged reading as an official selection in the Suncor Stage One Festival of New Canadian Work at the Lunchbox Theatre in Calgary in June 2018.

* * *

STEVEN looks around the stage.

STEVEN: Busy work, busy work, isn't that what you're supposed to do? The steps of mourning? . . . I know there's something about guilt and something else about acceptance . . . Which one is busy work?

He shakes a little, touches his face and arms. He feels his feet on the floor as if for the first time.

Weird.

He looks at his hands, rubs his chest. The doorbell rings. He ignores it.

He walks over to a suit and starts to put it on.

Pants, shirt half tucked in, barefoot, no jacket. That stays hanging.

The doorbell rings again.

STEVEN absently exits.

Enter JOANNE Denis. She has cleaning supplies with her that she leaves by the piano. She starts to pick up some of the clothing.

JOANNE: *(to herself)* Could you at least try to get these near a hamper?

STEVEN: *(offstage)* Hello?

JOANNE: Uh, Sorry. I rang the bell, no one / answered.

STEVEN: *(offstage)* Money's on the piano.

JOANNE: . . . Money's what? I haven't started yet. What?

Enter STEVEN half dressed in the suit. He was not expecting JOANNE and is immediately uncomfortable.

STEVEN: Oh . . . Hi.

JOANNE: Hi.

STEVEN walks to the piano and picks up an envelope.

STEVEN: I wasn't expecting you.

JOANNE: I didn't think I'd be back.

STEVEN: How much is it again? Is this awkward, me handing you money? I wasn't expecting you.

He turns away from her, distracted.

She takes a look at him partially dressed in the suit.

JOANNE: Good night last night?

STEVEN: Oh no, no, I'm trying it on, haven't worn it in a while.

JOANNE: Obviously, you have creases everywhere.

STEVEN: So, ah, how have you been?

JOANNE: I switched houses with Carol.

STEVEN: Yeah, Carol, she doesn't talk much.

JOANNE: She's been sick all week. That's why I'm here.

STEVEN: Why did you switch?

He walks to the hanging jacket, placing his feet very carefully on the floor.

JOANNE notices. He takes a breath.

JOANNE: What's the occasion?

STEVEN: I'm supposed to go to a funeral.

JOANNE: Oh, I'm sorry.

STEVEN: Ha. Okay.

JOANNE: That's funny?

STEVEN: No. It's, I'm just not sure *I'm* sorry.

JOANNE: That's a strange thing to say. Who died?

STEVEN: My father, last night.

She takes a few steps forward then stops herself.

JOANNE: Oh god, I'm sorry.

STEVEN: Stop saying that.

JOANNE: I should go. I can come back another time. / The dirt won't go anywhere.

STEVEN: No wait. Can you stay? It'll be nice to have someone else moving around in here.

JOANNE: Where's Sylvie?

STEVEN: She's not here.

JOANNE: . . . Did you tell her what happened?

STEVEN: Not yet.

JOANNE: Okay. But I'm gonna leave when she gets back.

STEVEN: Thanks.

    STEVEN stares at her.

JOANNE: What?

STEVEN: I'm glad you're here.

JOANNE: I'm not staying because of that. My mom died last year. I know what it's like.

STEVEN: Were you upset?

JOANNE: Of course I was upset. Who wouldn't be?

STEVEN: —

JOANNE: It's obvious you're upset.

STEVEN: Is it? Feels more like ambivalence . . . Do you want to know why I didn't tell / her?

JOANNE: No. You just told me your father died and you want to talk about . . . That's between you and your wife.

STEVEN: —

JOANNE: Was he sick?

STEVEN: Just—went. Not the healthiest of specimens.

JOANNE: Better it happens quick like that.

STEVEN: Really?

JOANNE: My mom was sick for a long time—you could see her just wanting to go.

STEVEN: But you got to say things?

JOANNE: When she would listen.

STEVEN: I don't think I'm going to go.

JOANNE: You have to, he was your father.

> *STEVEN moves toward the piano and steps heavily, like he's testing the floor. He shakes his legs before he sits.*

> *JOANNE watches him curiously.*

What was that?

STEVEN: What was what?

JOANNE: The stepping, the little jumps.

STEVEN: I don't know. I feel weird.

JOANNE: Yeah, your father died.

He wiggles his fingers out in front of him.

STEVEN: No, it's like I've forgotten what everything feels like.

JOANNE: Maybe I should start cleaning.

STEVEN: You don't have to.

JOANNE: No, it's . . . I have to pick up my daughter later.

STEVEN: Daughter? Really? How come I didn't know that?

JOANNE: You never asked.

STEVEN: Why wouldn't you just tell me something like that?

JOANNE: Would it have made a difference?

STEVEN: It's different . . . I guess you can't really know anyone.

JOANNE: I shouldn't be here. She'll be home soon right?

STEVEN: I'd like to talk about it.

JOANNE: About your dad or us or . . . ?

STEVEN: Why would I want to talk about my dad?

JOANNE: Because.

STEVEN: As far as I'm concerned, he died a long time ago.

Lights up on a restaurant table with three chairs. Sitting at the table, drinking a Manhattan, is PETER. *The father.*

We hear the sounds of a busy restaurant.

JOANNE: Then what's the problem?

STEVEN: There's no problem. I've made my peace. There's nothing I need *closure* with.

JOANNE: When was the last time you saw him?

STEVEN: About five years ago. Right after he got remarried. Gail.

JOANNE: That's a long time.

STEVEN walks over and sits down at the table.

STEVEN: Yeah . . . After the divorce I didn't see him much. We always went out for dinner, once, twice a year. He'd pick me up in his Lincoln Town Car or some other living room on wheels he had at the time and we'd find some German restaurant, maybe Italian, but usually Eastern European.

PETER: Wiener schnitzel, sauerbraten, goulash.

STEVEN: He had a few languages, so I'm not sure if it was because of the food or he liked to impress the staff by reading the menu out loud, pronouncing everything properly.

PETER: Topfenknödel.

STEVEN: He always ordered the schnitzel.

PETER: I'll have the schnitzel. You working?

JOANNE walks over and sits down at the table.

STEVEN: No matter how much I talked about it, he never knew what I was doing.

PETER: Still doing the, music stuff?

STEVEN: The same questions every single time.

JOANNE: Maybe he was trying to reach out. I wasn't married when I had my daughter, my mom stayed away for almost a year. She just didn't know how to deal with it.

PETER: It's a tough business. I used to know a few people who tried / to do it.

STEVEN: But you got to say what you needed to say. I never did—alive or dead.

STEVEN gets up and leans against the back of his chair, looking down at his father.

JOANNE: Then go, and say it.

STEVEN smirks, shakes his head, a little embarrassed with himself.

What's so funny?

STEVEN: I always wanted to lace into him right there at the restaurant . . . "I would have drowned if I didn't teach myself how to swim. You weren't around. You did nothing for me. I'm better off without you."

JOANNE: —

STEVEN: Well, that's what I would have wanted to say, but I would just cower. I would tell him I was thinking about going back to school, I'd try to find a "real" job . . . He was a big guy. I was a little scared of him.

STEVEN sits back down at the table.

But not the last time. He was slower, crooked, trouble with his back. I noticed it then for the first time, he was old.

PETER: You know what you'd be good at? Sales. You're so good with people. Gail noticed that immediately. She has a knack / for reading people.

STEVEN: I'm good with people? Fuck me! I hate people!! I'm a working musician, why couldn't he just accept it? I might not be rich but I do all right.

JOANNE: I'll say. Look at this place.

PETER: We should go somewhere and watch the game.

STEVEN: We used to communicate by watching hockey. That was our quality time. That's how I learned how to swear.

PETER: Oh for fuck sakes. Shoot the goddamn puck!!

STEVEN: That's why I can't watch a game anymore without feeling physically ill if the Canadiens are losing.

PETER: They don't have a real goal scorer. They need a Lafleur.

STEVEN: *Goddamnit shit!!* That was my favourite. Got sent to the principal's office in grade four for that one. So there we were, father and son, two musicians talking hockey because we couldn't talk about music, the one thing we had in common . . . I don't think he ever listened to my music.

JOANNE: What does it matter? You're making music, who cares if he listened or not?

STEVEN: Exactly! Why are you the only one that sees that!?

JOANNE: Don't pretend we know each other.

STEVEN: It's true. Sylvie was always defending him, "Give him a chance, he's trying, he just wants what best for you." Ahhh!

JOANNE: When's she / getting home?

STEVEN: What if you didn't get to patch things up with your mother?

JOANNE: I don't know if we really did. I think we just moved past it.

Lights up on LIZ, STEVEN's mother, smoking a cigarette. The sounds of suburbia fade in, birds, rustling trees, and the odd passing car.

STEVEN: Maybe it's better that way. After my parents got divorced, my mom told me everything.

LIZ: I didn't know what to do with boys. We talked about it, I'd raise your sister and he'd help with you.

STEVEN: It's strange. I only see her about once a year as well.

LIZ: I'm sorry.

STEVEN: . . . Have you ever had a parent apologize to you?

LIZ: He was supposed to teach you things. How to shave, tie a tie, drive, girls . . .

JOANNE: No, my mom never apologized. I think she wanted to but couldn't find the words.

STEVEN: Sometimes words shouldn't be found.

LIZ: I watched you get further and further away and I didn't know how to stop it.

JOANNE: When's Sylvie getting home?

STEVEN: She won't be back for a while.

STEVEN sits at the piano and plays a few chords, softly, and gets lost in the notes.

JOANNE lets him be and starts to sweep the floor in time to the melody.

LIZ: I was alone. I tried to do everything right, but it was never good enough. I always wondered what you kids saw when you looked at me . . . He was supposed to be there for you. When I tried, you pulled away. After that last fight you had with him, I knew you were gone. Blood on your face. I saw the blame. I didn't know what to do.

As STEVEN continues to play, JOANNE exits with the broom.

PETER: How's, what's her name, Sylvie is it?

LIZ: You were so angry all the time.

PETER: You two should come down to visit.

LIZ: Can you stay a little longer for Christmas this year?

PETER: Gail would love to see you again.

LIZ: Do you think he's really going to show up to your sister's wedding? He wouldn't just show up, would he?

PETER: Gail and I were talking about you two. She's good for you, eventually you'll start a family, no?

LIZ: He's just trying to make up for not showing up to yours.

STEVEN stops playing.

Lights down on LIZ and PETER. STEVEN feels his head and face, investigating.

AUDREY DWYER
CALPURNIA

Audrey Dwyer is a multi-disciplinary artist with over twenty years of experience working as an actor, director, playwright, teacher, artistic director, facilitator, and mentor. Audrey wrote and directed *Calpurnia*, which was produced by Nightwood Theatre and Sulong Theatre in 2018. The box-office hit was shown to sold-out audiences at Buddies in Bad Times Theatre. She is one of the winners of the CBC Creative Relief Fund to create a pilot TV show called *The Gordons*, which is inspired by *Calpurnia*. Her work has been recognized by the Cayle Chernin Awards and the Dora Mavor Moore Awards, and she has been twice nominated for the Pauline McGibbon Award for Direction. She was the Urjo Kareda artist-in-residence at Tarragon Theatre (2018/19) and was also the company's assistant artistic director. She is currently Associate Artistic Director of the Royal Manitoba Theatre Centre. She is a graduate of the National Theatre School.

Calpurnia is a satirical comedy, which features Julie Gordon, a young Jamaican-Canadian writer who is in the middle stages of adapting Harper Lee's *To Kill a Mockingbird* into a screenplay from the perspective of Calpurnia, the Finch family servant. Julie, a writer and budding activist, suffers from writer's block as her father, brother, and brother's white girlfriend celebrate her brother's success as a law graduate. In an argument, her brother informs her that she has no right to write about an African-American maid because she isn't Black enough. He accuses her of appropriating a culture she doesn't belong to. Julie decides to "do the work." *Calpurnia* ends with her realizing that in order to make change, she needs to check her values and how she shares her talents because change can only begin from within.

Calpurnia premiered in a production by Nightwood Theatre and Sulong Theatre in Toronto on January 17, 2018.

* * *

JULIE: Dad, I'm really busy right now.

LAWRENCE: You'll need to know this for tonight.

JULIE: Really busy.

LAWRENCE: Thompson is coming.

JULIE: I can't believe you gave him a "James Thompson" hook up.

LAWRENCE: All right.

JULIE: I can*not* believe you hooked Mark up with Thompson, Drader, and Associates.

LAWRENCE: Okay, quiet down.

JULIE: You move him from firm to firm to firm.

LAWRENCE: *(under his breath)* He's upstairs!

JULIE: He's more spoiled than I am.

LAWRENCE: *(under his breath)* Be! Quiet!

LAWRENCE checks to see if MARK is going to enter.

JULIE: This is unbelievable! You tell me when you hook *me* up.

LAWRENCE: You have less . . . pride.

JULIE: Wow.

LAWRENCE approaches JULIE.

LAWRENCE: Your brother's a man / **JULIE:** Oh my God.

LAWRENCE: Your brother's a man—

JULIE: Please please don't call him a man.

LAWRENCE: And men—

JULIE: It's weird, he's like, younger than me.

LAWRENCE: Men don't like to know they're being helped.

JULIE: I, like, taught him the alphabet, how to look both ways . . .

LAWRENCE: Okay.

JULIE: How to tie his shoelaces. You think he's ready to work with *James Thompson*?

LAWRENCE: He's more than ready.

JULIE: Doesn't look like it. / **LAWRENCE:** He's in a zone.

PRECY exits the kitchen.

JULIE: Two firms since graduation.

LAWRENCE: That's not so bad.

JULIE: Two. Firms. Since. Graduation.

LAWRENCE: *(firmly)* Sh!

He taps her with the article.

He can do better with a better firm.

JULIE: The article.

LAWRENCE: Yes?

JULIE: You hooked him up with the article too?

LAWRENCE: Yes. I did.

(under his breath) It's nothing major and Mark's feeling happy about it. Some kids need a little push.

JULIE: A little push?

PRECY enters with a carafe of red wine. She sets it on the countertop.

PRECY: Good Morning, Mr. Gordon. How are you today?

LAWRENCE: Tired. A bit of a headache, surprisingly.

JULIE: When are you going to let him grow a pair?

LAWRENCE: Pardon me?

JULIE: Oh, don't be bugged by that.

LAWRENCE: Can you get me some Aspirin please?

PRECY: Yes, Mr. Gordon.

LAWRENCE: Two.

PRECY: Yes, Mr. Gordon.

PRECY takes the clothing from the couch. She drapes the pieces over two chairs in the kitchen.

LAWRENCE: I don't recall any complaints when I *hooked you up* with Mike Goldberg.

JULIE: Whatever, Dad. It's a little different but whatever.

LAWRENCE: And how's that going?

JULIE: Great.

LAWRENCE: How much have you written since yesterday?

JULIE: I'm doing research.

LAWRENCE: Research?

JULIE: Yeah, research. Writers research.

LAWRENCE: Procrastinating?

JULIE: No.

LAWRENCE: Are you sure?

JULIE: *Yes.*

    LAWRENCE looks at her laptop.

LAWRENCE: You're on Facebook.

JULIE: So?

LAWRENCE: Facebook?

JULIE: There's a lot of information on Facebook.

LAWRENCE: Right.

JULIE: Tons of people are talking about what I'm writing about.

LAWRENCE: Black maids from the 1930s?

JULIE: Anti-racist policy. Race relations in the United States. Protests.

    PRECY enters with a tray, Aspirin on a plate and a glass of water.

LAWRENCE: Thank you, Precy.

    MARK enters.

PRECY: Oooh! Mark! Such good news!

MARK: Thanks, Precy.

PRECY: I read the article! Congratulations!

MARK: Thanks, Precy. Thanks a lot.

PRECY: Saturday newspaper? That is a big deal.

MARK: Thanks, Press.

PRECY: Do you want some lunch?

LAWRENCE: We're going biking shortly.

MARK: Water.

LAWRENCE: Water.

JULIE: Coffee.

> *PRECY exits, taking two champagne bottles. She puts them in the recycling bin. She prepares a cold compress for LAWRENCE. MARK sits at the table with JULIE.*

MARK: You should have partied with us last night.

JULIE: Yeah?

MARK: Dad brought out the good Scotch.

JULIE: Obviously.

LAWRENCE: A little headache.

MARK: It was the champagne.

PRECY enters with a cold compress for LAWRENCE on a tray. She takes three tumblers and the used napkin from the side table and exits into the kitchen.

LAWRENCE: I'm fine.

MARK: He's fine.

JULIE: Obviously.

MARK: What's your problem?

JULIE: I don't have a problem.

MARK: *(in Patois)* Yu no have no problem?

JULIE: Yep.

MARK: We kept you up.

JULIE: Yep.

MARK: You should have partied with us! We did shots.

JULIE: Obviously.

LAWRENCE: I did two shots.

MARK: Four shots but who's counting.

JULIE: Whatever. I'm doing some work here soooo . . .

MARK: Did you read my article?

JULIE: Nope.

MARK: Seriously?

JULIE: Yeah, I seriously didn't read your article.

MARK: You're coming to the dinner right?

JULIE: Maybe not.

MARK: (*standing, to* LAWRENCE) Julie has to come to the dinner.

LAWRENCE: She's coming.

JULIE: I'm probably not coming so you all need to just know that.

MARK: You have to read the article and you're coming to the dinner.

JULIE: Are you serious?

LAWRENCE: Julie.

MARK: I need all of us to be here for this. We're a team.

JULIE: I'm busy.

MARK looks at her computer screen.

MARK: No you're not.

JULIE: I'm writing. I have a deadline. I'm busy.

LAWRENCE: She'll be there.

CHRISTINE enters.

CHRISTINE: Jules! We missed you last night!

CHRISTINE tousles JULIE's hair.

Are you coming biking with us?

JULIE: Nope.

CHRISTINE: Are you kidding me? I never see you. It's gonna be quick!

CHRISTINE stretches. PRECY enters with water for MARK and LAWRENCE.

PRECY: Good Morning, Christine!

CHRISTINE: Precy! How are you?

PRECY: I'm very good, thank you. You look so nice.

CHRISTINE: Thanks, Press.

PRECY: Would you like some lunch?

LAWRENCE: I thought we'd have some lunch at the park.

PRECY: Would you like something to drink, Christine?

CHRISTINE: Hot water with a lemon slice would be the greatest, thank you. If you have a bit of fresh mint that would be great too.

PRECY *goes into the kitchen and turns the kettle on. She gets a* *lemon from a bowl filled with lemons, cuts it and puts a slice in a* *mug. She adds fresh mint from a glass filled with sprigs of mint.*

CHRISTINE: Not even a *little bit of biking?*

MARK: She's not going biking, she's not reading my article, and she's not coming to the dinner.

CHRISTINE: *(to* MARK*)* Oh baby, what are you saying?

MARK: She's not coming.

CHRISTINE: *(to* MARK*)* She'll be there.

MARK: Dad.

CHRISTINE: Jules. You have to come to the dinner—you just have to.

MARK: We need to be a family for this one.

CHRISTINE: You're all by yourself all the time.

JULIE: Okay, everyone, thanks for all the invitations to all the things. I have seven days to write this and I just want to write it. I *just* want to write it.

CHRISTINE: *(alarmed)* Are you coming to St. Barts?

JULIE: I'm not sure.

CHRISTINE: I paid for tickets.

JULIE: I know. I know you paid for the tickets, Christine.

CHRISTINE: I paid for the tickets, I mean I can change them that's fine but we're going to St. Barts, we always go to St. Barts.

JULIE: I know, I know we always go to St. Barts, I have a deadline I need to finish this, I have a week.

CHRISTINE: I can't believe we're not going to St. Barts.

LAWRENCE stands.

LAWRENCE: How's your treatment?

CHRISTINE: We're not going to St. Barts.

JULIE: My treatment is perfect.

CHRISTINE: Mark?

LAWRENCE: The script.

JULIE: It's . . . also . . . perfect.

LAWRENCE: What did Mike say about it?

JULIE: Calpurnia isn't active enough. Apparently a *common problem of female writers*. And she sounds too upper class. Apparently, she sounds too much like me. So, I'm doing research, watching *To Kill a Mockingbird* again. *Working*.

LAWRENCE: Research.

MARK and CHRISTINE have a moment together. CHRISTINE pulls away from MARK and sits away from him. She begins to read the article about him. They both read the article.

JULIE: I just need. Some time. To focus.

LAWRENCE: Are you bookmarking everything you come across? Because you should be bookmarking everything you come across. That laptop needs to be archiving every page you touch.

JULIE: Yeah, history does that.

LAWRENCE: You need to be creating an archive of all your research material.

LAWRENCE sits and takes over her laptop.

LAWRENCE: Are these your drafts?

Beat.

Do you have a file where you keep all of your drafts?

JULIE: I know how to make—

LAWRENCE: Here . . . we . . . go . . .

Beat.

And then you name it. *Calpurnia*?

JULIE: *Calpurnia.* Yes.

LAWRENCE: *(typing) Caaaalpuuuurnia.* There you go.

JULIE: Thank you.

LAWRENCE: Hard name to say. Drafts. In there.

JULIE: Thanks.

LAWRENCE stands.

LAWRENCE: And when you're brainstorming, do it on a big piece of paper. Write things down on a big piece of paper because you need to see what you'll be discussing in your work. Write the themes down, the conversations down. How it will go. Use different colored markers. A starburst approach. Write words. Lines.

Other words. Get up on your feet and write it. You're slumping like a . . . I'm signing you up for yoga.

LAWRENCE sits at her laptop.

JULIE: I'm not really into yoga.

MARK and CHRISTINE look up from their reading.

CHRISTINE: You love yoga.

JULIE: When I'm in those studios, I just wonder about who's there and who's not.

CHRISTINE: We're doing yoga in St. Barts.

JULIE: Ever wonder about who's there and who's not?

MICHAELA WASHBURN AND CARRIE COSTELLO
WATER UNDER THE BRIDGE

English, Irish, French, and Cree are the roots of this proud Métis artist who hails from Leduc, Alberta. Based in Ontario, Michaela Washburn is well versed in theatre, film, spoken word, hosting, clown, improvisation, stand-up, and workshop facilitation. An award-winning actor, Michaela also has multiple nominations, most notably for the Ontario Arts Council Indigenous Arts Award and the K.M. Hunter Artist Award for Theatre. Michaela's performance and written work has been shared internationally, including on stages in Wales, Aruba, and across Canada and the United States. At fifteen, Michaela won the Golden Poet Award in California, and has subsequently published in *Great Poems of Today*, *Queering the Way*, and *Theatre Passe Muraille: A Collective History*.

Carrie Costello loves adapting stories into theatre for young audiences. Inspired by a book or historical event, she begins figuring out the theatrical way in. Theatrical adaptations include *The Paperbag Princess*, *The Velveteen Rabbit*, and *There's a Mouse in my House*, which toured for three years throughout Ontario. Carrie co-wrote *Torn Through Time* with Frances Koncan and Cherissa Richards, which was produced in 2019 by Manitoba Theatre for Young People. Carrie and Michaela have teamed up with Joelle Peters to co-write *Frozen River*, which is scheduled to premiere in Winnipeg in 2021.

Sara and Waneek live on opposite sides of a river in 1812. They are from very different cultures and they are best friends. Once the war breaks out, Sara's cousin Daniel decides that no one is allowed to cross the river so he breaks the bridge. With the help of the audience, Sara and Waneek repair it and manage to convince Daniel that they do not have to fear people on the other side of the river.

Water Under the Bridge was first produced by Carousel Players in association with Castlemoon Theatre in St. Catharines, Ontario, on October 13, 2012.

* * *

DANIEL: Sara, look out. Waneek, you need to be the new guard.

WANEEK: (*to SARA*) Are you getting tired of this game?

DANIEL: It's not a game. It's dangerous over there, and with no lookout, no patrol, no guard to warn us, they could attack at any minute.

WANEEK: No one is going to attack. That's where I live. Those are our friends. Come on, Sara.

> *The girls begin to cross to WANEEK's side of the river. WANEEK makes it over the bridge, but SARA is left standing in the middle of the bridge.*

DANIEL: Wait. Wait! You live over there?!

WANEEK: Yeah.

DANIEL: Sara, get back! She's the enemy!

WANEEK: I'm not the enemy.

DANIEL: Yes you are.

WANEEK: No, I'm not.

SARA: Daniel, this game isn't fun.

DANIEL: It's not a game, Sara.

WANEEK: Well whatever it is, we're done playing.

DANIEL: I'm not playing. The message—

SARA: Yes?

DAD: Your dad sent me to—

SARA: What?

DANIEL: Your dad sent me to tell your mom that we are at war.

A beat.

WANEEK: What?

DANIEL: The secret message . . . is that the war has started.

SARA: War? You're making that up.

DANIEL: No I'm not. That's why your dad isn't home yet. That's why he sent me.

SARA: We're at war?

DANIEL: Yes.

WANEEK: What does that mean?

DANIEL: It means that this is the border and you're the enemy.

WANEEK: Just because I live over here?

DANIEL: Yes.

WANEEK: But we're friends and we trade.

DANIEL: Trading with you is treason.

SARA: Treason?

DANIEL: Trading with her means you are betraying our side.

WANEEK: But Sara and I are friends . . .

DANIEL: Maybe you were. But we're at war, and you live over there, and that makes you the enemy!

WANEEK: *We* are not at war and *I* am not the enemy. Just because this is the border and we live on different sides we're supposed to be enemies? That is ridiculous. We are friends. Best friends. Right, Sara?

No response.

Sara? Sara . . .

SARA: I don't know . . .

WANEEK turns away.

WANEEK: You don't know? Fine. Fine.

DANIEL: First give us back our rope.

WANEEK: What?

DANIEL: Give us back our rope.

SARA: Daniel . . .

WANEEK: A trade is a trade.

DANIEL: Fine, then here are your hides.

DANIEL goes to the middle of the bridge.

Take them.

WANEEK: You can't go back on a trade.

DANIEL: Here.

DANIEL throws the hides.

Now give us back our rope.

WANEEK: (*to SARA*) Are you going to let him do this? Fine, here.

She throws the rope at DANIEL.

And take your eggs back too.

WANEEK goes onto the bridge and tries to hand SARA the basket of eggs, but SARA does not take it.

SARA: Just keep them.

WANEEK: No. Take them back.

SARA: I don't want them.

WANEEK: I don't want them either. Here.

WANEEK drops the basket at SARA's feet.

SARA: You broke them.

WANEEK: I don't care!

WANEEK storms off the bridge to her side of the river.

SARA: Fine.

SARA begins taking WANEEK's laundry off the line.

Then I suppose you'll want this back too.

SARA begins tossing the clothes across the river. The first piece makes it.

WANEEK: What are you doing?

SARA: Giving your clothes back.

SARA tosses another piece, it makes it.

Catch! Catch. Oh and this too.

SARA throws tóta's bag next, but it doesn't make it and falls in the river. WANEEK gasps. SARA looks horror-struck, WANEEK as well.

SARA: I'm sorry. I'm sorry.

A beat.

Waneek, I'm really sorry. Please, I didn't mean to throw it in the river.

She waits for a response.

I didn't, really. Please, I'm sorry. I'll make you a new one.

WANEEK: My tóta made that, Sara.

SARA: I know, I'm so sorry. What can I do?

No response.

WANEEK stands staring at the river, almost in tears.

It's just that . . .

SARA sits down miserably.

DANIEL: It's just a bag, Sara.

SARA: No it's not. Her grandmother gave her that bag before she passed away and I just threw it in the river.

DANIEL: It was an accident.

SARA: It doesn't matter. Those things Granddad gave you?

DANIEL: Yah.

SARA: Think of how you feel about them . . .

DANIEL: Yah.

SARA: What if I threw them in the river? Yah.

SARA begins gathering up the rest of WANEEK's clothes and putting them in the basket.

Waneek, I'm really sorry.

SARA approaches the bridge.

Here.

DANIEL: You can't do that.

DANIEL stands in her way.

SARA: Daniel just let me give her these clothes.

DANIEL: It's treason, Sara.

SARA: This isn't a trade.

DANIEL: You still can't cross.

SARA: Those clothes belong to her akhwá:tsire!

DANIEL: Her what?

SARA: Her family. And I'm giving them back.

> As SARA *attempts to go to the bridge with the basket,* DANIEL *stops her.*

DANIEL: No you're not!

> DANIEL *takes the basket from* SARA.

SARA: Daniel, give those back. They belong to Waneek.

> DANIEL *puts down the basket and unties one of the ropes from the nearest post of the bridge.*

What . . . Daniel, no. Daniel, stop it. What are you . . . Daniel, what are you doing?

DANIEL: I'm closing this bridge.

> DANIEL *crosses the bridge and removes a rope from* WANEEK's *side of the bridge.*

WANEEK: You can't do that!

> *The bridge breaks in the middle.* DANIEL *falls.*

DANIEL: Help!

PRESENT

PATTI FLATHER
PARADISE

Award-winning playwright Patti Flather grew up in North Vancouver, BC, and now she creates theatre in the spectacular Yukon. Her plays include *Sixty Below* (with Leonard Linklater), *West Edmonton Mall, Where the River Meets the Sea, Street Signs* (formerly *The Soul Menders*), and *Paradise*, and the devised creations *Go Angel Girlfriends, Tell Me More . . .* , and *Map of the Land, Map of the Stars*. Patti co-founded and was the artistic director of Gwaandak Theatre until 2019. She's a recipient of the Yukon Arts Builder Award and a past winner of Theatre BC's national playwriting competition, and with her husband Leonard Linklater is the inaugural recipient of the Borealis Prize: The Commissioner of Yukon Award for Literary Contribution. She has an M.F.A. in Creative Writing from the University of BC and is a dramaturg, director, educator, and fiction and screenwriter. She's currently working on her first novel. Patti lives in Whitehorse.

After a traumatic assault in Central America, Rachel returns home, but it isn't the reprieve she expected. She comes back to turmoil between her parents, and a part-time job in her dad's medical office. Her father, George, full of endearing blunder, tries unsuccessfully to connect with his daughter, who seems to be reeling. Her childhood friend Khalil isn't around to provide support. He's in Afghanistan travelling and volunteering when he is wrongfully arrested. On the periphery is Wally—off work because of a logging injury—who spends a great deal of time in George's office. Wally struggles to buy food for his dog Lucky, his rent payments are overdue, and the ringing in his ears just won't stop. He's looking for help in all the right places, but nobody seems to notice he's deteriorating until it's too late.

Paradise premiered at the Yukon Arts Centre in Whitehorse, Yukon, in March 2015 as a production of Gwaandak Theatre and MT Space, in association with the Yukon Arts Centre.

* * *

KHALIL is in prison. RACHEL enters, in a happy partying mood. It's late, after a night drinking and dancing. A tourist hassles her.

KHALIL: I'm healthy. I don't need a checkup. I don't have nasty crotch bugs. I don't—no girlfriend. No.

RACHEL: I said okay, that was fun and all, whoop-whoop. But good night, Simon from Sudbury. I said I'm tired. I'm going back to the hostel. I'm catching the chicken bus first thing.

KHALIL: Why is the lady soldier here? It's not funny. Don't point like that. I'm not a girl. I'm not a faggot.

RACHEL: Okay, goodbye. Look, I have a boyfriend, okay? Dressed like what? Give me a break. I'm not a cocktease.

KHALIL: I'm not the little bitch.

RACHEL: I'm not a slut.

KHALIL: I don't have AIDS; I never . . .

RACHEL: Quit following me. You're worse than the locals.

KHALIL: Please put that stick away.

RACHEL: Leave me alone. Get away, you creep. Stop. Don't.

KHALIL: Why are you doing this? I'm not dirty. Please.

RACHEL: Don't you have a mother?

KHALIL: Please. Not there.

> *KHALIL is forced to bend over for a brutal rectal examination. He
> screams in agony. RACHEL is sexually assaulted in an alley by the
> tourist.*

RACHEL: I won't cry for you.

Pause.

Skin.

KHALIL: Flying.

RACHEL: Peeling.

KHALIL: Soaring.

RACHEL: Scraping.

KHALIL: Wings.

RACHEL: Shedding.

KHALIL: Feathers.

RACHEL: Red.

KHALIL: Softly.

RACHEL: Raw.

KHALIL: Landing. Where am I?

    Beat.

Nana?

RACHEL: (*feels for her locket*) My locket.

KHALIL: Does anyone know where I am?

RACHEL: Por favor. I need to phone Canada right now.

KHALIL: I need to call my grandmother.

RACHEL: (*to phone*) Pick up, please, come on.

KHALIL: I need a doctor.

GEORGE: Hello? Sheila?

RACHEL: Dad?

    Beat.

I need to talk to you.

GEORGE: Who's there?

RACHEL: It's me, Rachel.

GEORGE: Hello? Who is this?

RACHEL: Can't you hear me? Dad!

GEORGE: I can't hear you.

RACHEL: But I can hear you. Talk to me, Dad. I still have my locket.

GEORGE: Is this a prank call?

RACHEL: It's not a prank. Wait. Keep talking. Dad. How's Mom and Pooks?

GEORGE: Goodbye.

RACHEL: No, don't hang up.

GEORGE retreats.

Scrape it clean.

KHALIL: I can't.

WALLY enters. He's at home with Lucky.

WALLY: Come here, buddy. Lucky! There's my boy. You want a little scratch? Sure you do. Oh, that feels good. Kisses for Daddy. Look at your corkscrew tail wagging, like a windup toy. Just like when I found you behind the dumpster. Soaking wet, trembling like a poplar leaf, your ribs sticking out. You still had enough in ya to wag that tail, didn't ya? I rescued you. Yes, I did. You like that story, don't ya?

Beat.

We're gonna be okay.

Beat.

What's that? You want to sit in my lap? Come on then. That's my little guy.

RACHEL: Read me a bedtime story, okay? The bear of little brain.

GEORGE: Winnie-the-Pooh.

KHALIL hears the sounds of prison.

KHALIL: Stop the sound echoes. Wind. Leg irons. Boots. Men and boys rattling thin wire cages. Puking. Crying. Screaming. Find a way out. Find it now. Lizards. Hedgehogs. Snakes.

RACHEL opens her locket. She examines it, then holds the locket to her heart. She puts it away.

I found it. Okay, we're going through the portal arch. Let's go.

KHALIL leads RACHEL into a childhood flashback. She holds a shoebox.

What are you doing?

RACHEL: I'm catching snakes.

KHALIL: Why?

RACHEL: To scare people, obviously. Open the box for me.

He hesitates.

It's a garter snake. It won't bite.

He opens the box.

Who are you?

KHALIL: Khalil.

RACHEL: I'm Rachel. Let's go make somebody old pee their pants.

They play a game, revealing the snake in the box to frighten each other, then exchanging roles. They are playful, free, and full of laughter.

KHALIL: Maybe we're scaring him. Nana—my grandma—says "be kind to all creatures."

RACHEL: We'll build Snake World to make him safe and happy.

KHALIL: Okay. Blades of grass.

RACHEL: Moss.

KHALIL: Leaves.

RACHEL: Tons of places to play and sleep.

KHALIL: And dream.

RACHEL and KHALIL become adults again. RACHEL packs her belongings to leave Central America.

RACHEL: *(exiting)* Adios.

JOEL FISHBANE
IN THE YICHUD ROOM

Joel Fishbane is an award-winning author of fiction, non-fiction, theatre, and film. His novel *The Thunder of Giants* is available from St. Martin's Press, while his other work has been honoured and performed at festivals, contests, and conferences across Canada, the United States, and overseas. For production rights and other info please visit www.joelfishbane.net

At a traditional Jewish wedding, the "yichud" occurs right after the ceremony, during which the bride and groom are isolated for a period of reflection and prayer. When Amy and Sutler are sequested in their yichud room, however, things go awry after a mysterious stranger arrives bearing news from Sutler's past.

In the Yichud Room was first produced at Alumnae Theatre's New Ideas Festival, Toronto, on March 10, 2004.

* * *

SUTLER enters. He stops when he sees CHESTERTON.

AMY: (*to audience*) Sutler came in a moment later. You should have seen his face. I have never seen anything collapse like that. He suddenly looked very small and he staggered a bit, and dropped the beer in his hand and spilt it all over the carpet. I remember thinking, "They're going to charge me for the cleaning." Such absurdities. I kept staring at the beer as it seeped into the carpet, I barely heard the explanation, something about her sending a letter, I was hardly listening because I kept looking at the beer and thinking that this would be the last time I would ever see Sutler spill beer.

She stays there as the scene continues

SUTLER: She's alive?

CHESTERTON: And ready to cakewalk all along the Champs-Élysées. She's here. We just have to get her to Paris.

SUTLER: We?

CHESTERTON: Yes. Both of us. She wants to go, it's tradition, you know. You'll have to pay, of course. I don't have much, I'm on welfare.

SUTLER: She sent you a letter.

CHESTERTON: That's right. Such wonderful grammar too and she spelt everything properly, I taught her myself, did she ever tell you that?

SUTLER: All the time. She said you used those magnets you stick on refrigerators.

CHESTERTON: (*laughs, delighted*) Yes! Yes! Exactly!

AMY: *(to audience)* It was so strange, it was as if I wasn't even in the room and I was catching a glimpse of the old Sutler, the one who Mr. Chesterton had described, the Sutler I never knew or met.

SUTLER: *(smiling to himself)* Sandra.

AMY: How badly he loved her, I thought.

SUTLER: Sandra.

AMY: I could see it when he spoke her name. I marvelled at it. Here was a Sutler I had never seen before and would probably never see again. The one who didn't drink and stayed up all night reading Christopher Isherwood.

SUTLER: How did she ever find you?

CHESTERTON: Oh, she's smart, our Sandra, you know she is. She found a way.

SUTLER: How?

CHESTERTON: Tracked me down, somehow, you shouldn't ask so many questions, boy, Sandra is alive, who cares about the details? Sandra's alive and she's ready to cakewalk. Remember that night you two did the cakewalk in our living room?

SUTLER: That was many years ago.

CHESTERTON: Funny, I think of it every day. Every day, and it makes me laugh, you and Sandra, and now you'll be together all over again.

AMY: (*to audience*) I was in shock. Sutler doing a cakewalk, you saw him, he wouldn't even dance with me. And what's that glint in his eye, do you see it? It's never there. This fucking jealousy rose up inside me.

CHESTERTON: We can be there tomorrow. Tomorrow, Sutler, do you know the first thing, the first thing she said, was that I should find you.

SUTLER: She said that?

CHESTERTON: First thing.

AMY: (*to audience*) First thing. I tried to picture this girl, this Sandra, roaming around, thinking of Sutler, thinking of my husband, and I felt absurdly betrayed as if he had been cheating on me.

SUTLER: God, I loved her.

AMY: (*to audience*) He was going to go. Why shouldn't he? I felt so horrid, how we had spent our only minutes of marriage arguing with each other. Probably the only time I'll ever be married and look at how I wasted it. We didn't even consummate it. In the eyes of God we weren't even married. In the eyes of God we were nothing.

SUTLER: Can I see the letter?

CHESTERTON: (*faltering slightly*) What?

SUTLER: Can I see the letter?

CHESTERTON: I, uh, don't seem to have it on me.

SUTLER: Where would you have left it?

CHESTERTON: Probably in my other pants. Which I had to sell to get train fare up here, so you see, I don't have the letter—

SUTLER: William. There was a letter, wasn't there?

CHESTERTON: Of course. Of course there was. We have to leave, right away. Right away, Sutler.

SUTLER: Where is she now? We have to get to Paris, right? So where is she?

CHESTERTON: She's here, she's here.

SUTLER: In the city?

CHESTERTON: (faltering) We need to get her to Paris. It's tradition.

SUTLER: William.

CHESTERTON: I got a letter.

SUTLER: No. You didn't.

CHESTERTON: Sutler, please—

SUTLER: I'm married, now. I'm going on my honeymoon.

CHESTERTON: Honeymoon! With who? With, this, this *thing?*

SUTLER: I'm sorry, William.

CHESTERTON: Yes, here it is, I did get a letter.

CHESTERTON *produces a letter.*

SUTLER: Let me see it.

CHESTERTON: Why can't you just trust me?

SUTLER: *William.*

SUTLER takes the letter.

CHESTERTON: It came to me last week.

AMY: Dear Mr. Chesterton, it said.

CHESTERTON: It was in the dead letter office. And that's what it was—

AMY: We regret to inform you—

CHESTERTON: —a *dead* letter—

AMY: —a body was recently found—

CHESTERTON: —some nut decided to deliver all the dead letters—

AMY: —it has been positively identified—

CHESTERTON: —fucking do-gooders.

SUTLER: (*to audience*) It didn't come as much of a shock. Like if God came down, you'd think "Well there, you see, I was right." I could have done without the details, mind you.

(*to CHESTERTON*) I'm so sorry, William.

CHESTERTON: Don't say that. I hate it. Every day, people looking at me with sad looks and saying how sorry they are. "Oh look, let me help you," they say. "Oh look, I found a *letter*." Why couldn't you just believe me? We could have been in . . . look, we have the flat, we'll stay there, it's just for a year, you can come back and marry this girl all over again.

SUTLER: I'm sorry William. I promised her I'd only marry her once.

CHESTERTON: Then to hell with you. She deserves better than you, deserves better than to just be forgotten. What am I supposed to do? I have to go get her.

SUTLER: I don't understand.

AMY: Sandra's body had been waiting. In the letter it said you had sixty days to claim it, but the letter was almost five years old. They had buried the body in a public cemetery.

CHESTERTON: They just threw her in the ground.

AMY: Pauper's funeral.

CHESTERTON: Like she meant nothing.

AMY: He wanted her cremated.

CHESTERTON: She deserves to be in Paris.

AMY: He wanted her ashes thrown from the Eiffel Tower.

CHESTERTON: And here you are getting married.

AMY: I didn't know what to do. There were two men, mine and Sandra's. The one who didn't drink and the one who does; the one who reads Christopher Isherwood and the one who doesn't; the one who was married to me . . . and the one who loved Sandra Chesterton. I thought, this can only end badly. But it didn't.

(*to* SUTLER *and* CHESTERTON) What if we took her to Paris?

SUTLER: You mean . . .

AMY: What if we brought her to Paris?

CHESTERTON: Why would you do that?

AMY: Because my husband loved her. And because it's tradition.

SUTLER: It's not mine. It's his.

AMY: (*to audience*) Sutler was right. It was Mr. Chesterton's tradition. So we offered to take him along.

CHESTERTON: You would take me to Paris.

AMY: You'd have to clean yourself up.

CHESTERTON: But it's your honeymoon.

AMY: Well we won't keep you around for the whole time.

    AMY *leads* CHESTERTON *out.*

SUTLER: (*to audience*) Once we were alone, I didn't know what to say. I kept thinking, what if Sandra had been alive? What if she wanted me back? What would I have done? I have no idea what I would have done. She was such a long time ago. We were so young.

AMY *returns.*

SUTLER: I should have said something.

AMY: What would you have said?

SUTLER: I could have told you.

AMY: Told me what? That you were in love once? We've all been in love once. Why do we try to pretend that we haven't been hurt?

SUTLER: I don't like you knowing that I loved someone else.

AMY: You loved her that much?

SUTLER: Yes.

AMY: And you still fell in love with me?

SUTLER: Yes.

AMY: I think that's the most romantic thing I've ever heard.

SUTLER: I'll tell you everything, if you want to hear it.

AMY: I do. But not now. We only have twenty minutes.

SUTLER: What do you want to do?

AMY: Well it's the yichud room, isn't it? Help me out of this dress.

They kiss.

* * *

AMY and SUTLER separate and go into their respective spotlights.

AMY: Marriage.

SUTLER: Marriage.

AMY: The world's oldest profession.

SUTLER: The ultimate tradition.

AMY: Centuries old.

BOTH: Marriage.

AMY: We waited until the hour was up.

SUTLER: Once it was finished, we went out.

AMY: People called me Mrs. Brody.

SUTLER: They called her Mrs. Brody.

AMY: I didn't correct them.

SUTLER: I did.

AMY: Marriage is about compromise, you know.

Curtain.

MICHAELA DI CESARE
SUCCESSIONS

Michaela is a playwright-performer with a master's degree in Drama from the University of Toronto. As an actor, theatre credits include *Winter's Daughter* (Tableau D'Hôte Theatre/Segal Studio), *Gratitude* (MainLine Theatre), *A Bear Awake in Winter* (Next Stage Theatre Festival), *Birds of a Feather* (Roseneath Theatre), *Urban Tales* (Centaur Theatre/Urbi et Orbi), *A Midsummer Night's Dream* (Humber River Shakespeare), and *State of Denial* (Teesri Duniya Theatre). Michaela performed her one-woman show *8 Ways my Mother was Conceived* across North America. Michaela wrote and performed in *In Search of Mrs. Pirandello* in the 2016 WildSide Festival at Centaur Theatre, which also produced a mainstage production of *Successions* (Outstanding New Text, METAS 2018). Her play *Extra/Beautiful/U* won first place in the 2017 Write-on-Q! competition presented by Infinithéâtre. Her latest play, *FOMO*, premiered with Geordie Theatre in September 2019, and she was Playwright-in-Residence at Centaur Theatre for the 2019/2020 season, working on *Terroni or Once Upon a Time in the South*.

Successions is a family saga about two second-generation Italian Canadian brothers. Anthony is an uptight, upwardly mobile lawyer running for office with a campaign managed by his wife, Cristina, a successful television performer. Enzo is the younger brother who has always stayed close to home. Nat met Enzo nine months ago at a club and is currently eight months pregnant. After the sudden death of their parents, Anthony and Enzo must decide whether to hold on to the family home, a rundown relic stuffed to the gills with memories, secrets, and a lifetime of worthless junk. To move forward they need to let go, but at what cost to their relationship?

Successions was first produced by Centaur Theatre Company, Montreal, on April 10, 2018.

* * *

NAT: Okay. I gotta ask. What's this campaign? Like, I keep seeing your enormous face on the way to Rouge—

CRISTINA: You're still clubbing?

ANTHONY: It's an election, Nat.

ANTHONY notices that ENZO is still upset.

(doing a Barney Gumble impression) Oh no, an election! That's one of those deals where they close the bars, isn't it?

ENZO: (doing a Mr. Burns impression) Ironic, isn't it, Smithers? This anonymous clan of slack-jawed troglodytes has cost me the election, and yet if I were to have them killed, I would be the one to go to jail.

The brothers chuckle and high-five one another.

CRISTINA: Who are they now?

NAT: It's old school Simpsons.

CRISTINA: Oh.

NAT: So, Ant is gonna be mayor? Like Mayor Quimby.

CRISTINA: It's not a mayoral election. It's a federal election. For a seat in Ottawa.

NAT: A seat. Okay. Mayor sounds better.

CRISTINA: (to *NAT*) Anthony pleaded a big case at the Supreme Court last year. And he won.

ENZO: Oh yeah. That was cool. All my friends were like, that's so cool.

CRISTINA: He overturned a Quebec Court of Appeal judgment that allowed smoking in multi-unit dwellings. When the judgment banning smoking was published, all three major parties were vying to have this star represent them.

NAT: Wow. Look how proud she is.

CRISTINA: I am. Look at him. He's my work of art. My Galatea. My Eliza Doolittle.

NAT: Huh? Your what?

ANTHONY: Cristina, I've told you before. This shtick is very embarrassing.

ENZO: Better she gets it out of her system now than in the interview.

CRISTINA: I got his cholesterol down from seven point two—seven point two can you believe it? It was through the roof when we met—I got it down to two point eight five. That's the dairy-free, gluten-free diet we're on. Plus the speech coaching, the fashion consulting—

ANTHONY: Okay, Cris.

NAT: Sounds like you did a lot for poor little Ant from the wrong side of the Met. It's too bad he totally threw your career under the bus.

CRISTINA: Many women put their careers on hold when they want to have children. Why is it any different if I take a year or two off to assist Anthony in this transition?

ANTHONY: Right, and I made sacrifices to help her when she was just starting out as an actress.

CRISTINA: What sacrifices?

ANTHONY: No, I just meant . . . going to theatre stuff, sitting on boards . . . being civil to a lot of horrible people.

ENZO: This guy went to see so many fucking plays. When they started dating, I was like, "Bro, I hope you're getting some or it's not even worth it." And he was like, "Bro, she's a virgin!"

CRISTINA: You told him that?

ANTHONY: I don't recall . . .

ENZO: Bey yeah, we were smoking—

ANTHONY: I. Don't. Recall.

ENZO: Oh, you don't, eh? You forget every conversation we ever had in here? Just wiped it all clean from your head? Wiped the whole place clean.

ANTHONY: You think I don't know when I walk into a courtroom that I carry this place on my back? Do you know how many racist colleagues made mafia insinuations, to my face, in court, when I was just starting out?

NAT: Racism? Is he joking right now?

CRISTINA: You mean prejudiced colleagues, Ant, not racists.

ANTHONY: What I mean is I had none of the advantages of growing up crooked—no money, no influence, no connections—but I had all the disadvantages of my Italian roots. You know how many times they'd have me spell my name for the stenographer? "Maitre D-d-duh si-si-sicky-o" and I'm repeating Di Ciccio over and over. Finally, I just started walking right over to the stenographer and handing her a business card. It's an advantage right off the bat to have an easy to pronounce, francophone name—like Trudeau. Not to mention the nepotistic advantage.

ENZO: Oh my god. Your disadvantages. I'm so sorry that your ethnic name and your tan face are such fuckin inconvenient inheritances. It's not like I inherited a disability—

ANTHONY: A neurological condition.

ENZO: Yeah. It's no surprise the brother with ADHD couldn't become a lawyer. And meanwhile you, you fuckin stole my Ritalin to help you study for exams.

ANTHONY: Oh please. I told you you could have got into any program—even med school at McGill—by playing the disability card. You chose to play the victim instead. You chose to be stoned all the time.

NAT: He's better when he's stoned.

ENZO: It's okay, Nat. My brother just has a chip on his shoulder because he didn't get into McGill. He had to struggle and speak French over at U of M.

ANTHONY: I couldn't afford to go to McGill. I lost a scholarship because our parents' taxes weren't up to date.

ENZO: It's really easy for you to shit on our childhood and talk about carrying it on your back. Really? Where? I don't see it. You were able to throw on a suit and leave us all behind.

CRISTINA: Anthony has problems too.

ANTHONY: Cristina—

CRISTINA: No. I'm tired of them always acting like you won the lottery. I don't know everything that went down here—but Anthony clearly has some post-traumatic stress. He has nightmares and panic attacks.

ENZO: Aw poor you, Ant. That must be tough. You have bad dreams and panic attacks like a pussy.

CRISTINA: I don't agree with trivializing panic attacks and using a pejorative word for the female anatomy to further stigmatize and gender mental illness /

ENZO: What the fuck is she even talking about? Jesus, Ant. You make your wife believe we're such dirt. Mommy and Daddy were not the worst parents in the world. They didn't gamble away our house or get divorced.

ANTHONY: Look around you! This is an addiction. And they should have divorced. That's what I wanted.

CRISTINA: It wasn't your decision to make.

ENZO: Step-parents suck, Ant. We would have been molested. Locked in closets and shit.

ANTHONY: Or maybe we'd still have all the money Dad spent as penance for his sins.

ENZO: We were poor. You don't get to be angry just because we were poor.

ANTHONY: We shouldn't have been. That's the point!

ENZO: Nonno got sick. Daddy had to close the business. They had bad luck.

ANTHONY: There is no such thing as bad luck! Not here. Not in Canada. You make your own luck.

NAT: Yup. Hashtag self-made.

ENZO: But what's the big fucking deal? We had food. We had clothes. We had a roof. We were fine. You were the one, fuckin eighteen years old, sitting on the floor of the closet crying because you couldn't handle . . . what? I don't even know . . . being good at everything?

ANTHONY: You don't know. You were always protected from everything because you had a "learning disability." You know, getting stoned and never studying.

ENZO: Ah shut up, you were so jealous of me you went and invented your own "disability." You couldn't even let me have that.

ANTHONY: What?

ENZO: You fuckin started pretending you couldn't see people.

ANTHONY: I didn't make that up.

ENZO: You gave it some bullshit name. Prissy piss whatever.

CRISTINA: Prosopagnosia.

ANTHONY: Cristina.

NAT: Pro-so-what?

CRISTINA: Face blindness.

NAT: You can't see my face?

Beat. ANTHONY *doesn't reply.*

NAT: YOU CAN'T SEE MY FACE?

ANTHONY: I have a mild form of the neurological condition. I can learn faces I see often, but it's difficult. If I don't see someone for a while, I forget. Today, the only face I know is the one I wake up next to every day—

ANTHONY *is being sentimental.* CRISTINA *cracks up.*

CRISTINA: It's why he needs me at networking events! I'm such a cliché political wife, I need to whisper in his ear, "This is Maitre so-and-so."

ENZO: He was always calling my friend Tim Sam and Sam Tim.

ANTHONY: Tim and Sam went through a long phase of getting the same haircut and wearing the same clothes. Assholes.

NAT: Wait. Wait. What if you run into people, like on the street?

ANTHONY: It can get awkward, but there are other clues I can piece together: body size, gait, tone of voice, clothing.

CRISTINA: It's why he never noticed all his exes were ugly. Those girls took advantage of his impairment.

NAT: Mii. And here she was a minute ago being all, "bla bla female pussy power bla bla."

ENZO: Wait a minute . . . they *were* ugly . . . so this thing is real?

ANTHONY: Why would I make up such a stupid weakness?

ENZO: I thought you wanted to be more like me. For a change.

NAT: But like, what do you see instead of a face?

ENZO: Babe, there's no instead of, there's just no face. Right?

ANTHONY: Not exactly.

ENZO: Like the invisible man. You just see hairstyles floating on top of clothes.

ANTHONY: No.

CRISTINA: There's a famous case of prosopagnosia where the man's brain replaced all faces with other objects.

NAT: Aha! So you do replace the face.

ANTHONY: In some cases.

CRISTINA: This man thought his wife was a hat.

ENZO: Do you think your wife is a hat, Ant?

NAT: More importantly, what kind of hat? I'd go with beanie.

ANTHONY: All cases of prosopagnosia are different! I do not see hat people.

NAT: Then what do you see?

ANTHONY: It's sort of like . . .

CRISTINA: Lego people.

ENZO: What?

ANTHONY: The features are broad, cartoonish, kind of two-dimensional.

ENZO: Oh man! It's like you're living in Legoland. That's so cool.

ANTHONY: It's hard, Enzo. I always worry I'm going to ignore the wrong person. And I suck at non-verbal—what's the thing you always tell me, Cristina?

CRISTINA: Non-verbal cues. Subtle facial expressions are totally lost on him.

ANTHONY: Yeah.

CRISTINA: But I help. Those are kind of my specialty.

ANTHONY: Yet another thing for which I am indebted to you, right?

CRISTINA: I wasn't saying it like that.

ENZO: So, we're both kind of messed up, eh?

ANTHONY: It's all genetic.

CRISTINA: It's one of the many reasons we chose not to have children.

NAT: If one parent has ADHD the kid has more than a 50% chance of having it too. So what? It's not like my kid will be retarded. We did those tests.

CRISTINA: I didn't say retarded. I wouldn't say retarded.

NAT: I'm sorry, but all you PC people. You hashtag-body-shaming people. You bully bulliers. You're really starting to get on my nerves. Being PC is just not saying true shit. I prefer to be honest.

ANTHONY: It's like how Rita got depressed all the time. It's something with the way the nerves work in our brains.

ENZO: No way. Depressed. What are you saying? Mommy was just overwhelmed. She was working all day at the hospital, raising us, and taking care of Nonno. And he wasn't easy. The scratching, the yelling—he'd bite her sometimes.

CRISTINA: I saw him pinch her butt once.

ANTHONY: I begged her to get help. I guess in her own way, she finally did.

CRISTINA: What are you saying?

ANTHONY: Come on, the accident. Am I the only one who sees it?

ENZO: Dad fell asleep. He's been falling asleep at the wheel for as long as I can remember.

NAT: That's not a normal thing.

ENZO: He was always exhausted. He worked double shifts every day.

ANTHONY: Yet somehow never had any money . . .

ENZO: The point is he was a disaster on the road. The number of times he totalled the car by driving off the shoulder . . . it was kind of his thing.

NAT: He should have lost his licence!

ENZO: Nah, driving with him was always a blast! You'd just have Mom yelling at him to keep him awake, "Louie, ARE YOU ASLEEP?" And then he'd yell back, "WOMAN, YOU SCARED ME! YOU WANT ME TO DRIVE RIGHT OFF THE HIGHWAY?"

ANTHONY: I know he fell asleep. I'm not arguing that. I just think this time she let him. She thought up the perfect punishment for a horrible son like me.

CRISTINA: She wasn't punishing . . . anyone.

ENZO: Shit. Shit. That's fucked up. You're saying she just let him drive off the road? Jesus, fuck.

ENZO circles the room as though to clear the air and addresses the painting.

ENZO: Did you do that, Mommy? Did you let him? You let him?

NAT: You're upsetting my bae and my baby!

ANTHONY: It was just a theory. I—

ENZO: Why would you say something like that?

ANTHONY: Look, forget it. I'm buzzed that's all. And I'm buzzed because I did what you wanted. We smoked, we drank, now please come take a look at the documents.

ENZO: Yeah. Okay. Whatever.

ENZO joins ANTHONY at the desk where the papers are.

ANTHONY: There is a grace period in which successors can renounce. Currently, we are in a holding period during which the succession is frozen.

ENZO: Oh. My. God. Remember Dash?

ANTHONY: Dash?

ENZO: Dash the frozen cat.

ANTHONY: Oh, yeah.

NAT: You guys had a cat?

ENZO: Yeah, Dash—

ANTHONY: We had cats. Plural. My mother, despite her son's cat allergy, asthma, and chronic bronchitis, took in every stray that turned up.

ENZO: You're telling it wrong. Fuck. Too many "cry me a river" moments. So Dash, the cat, died in our house. It was winter so Daddy says he's going to go outside and bury him in the snow.

NAT: No.

ENZO: Yeah, and he even added a couple of shovelfuls of snow on top every day as the weather got warmer. So the cat's buried. Whatever. We have two or three others at home.

ANTHONY: More like six.

ENZO: Spring comes and the snow starts to melt. And you could start to see the stuff that was under there.

ANTHONY: Toilet seats, car engines, things Louie had long forgotten he even brought home.

ENZO: So we're coming home from school one day and we just see this thing sticking up out of the snow.

NAT: No!

ENZO: And we don't realize what it is yet.

ANTHONY: I did. You didn't.

ENZO: So I go pull on it and I pull up a fuckin frozen cat. A whole cat that's still kind of in this block of ice—like a popsicle.

NAT: Ew! Then what?

ENZO: Dad said to leave him there till everything was melted—

ANTHONY: Like that was his plan all along.

ENZO: And then he buried him in the actual ground.

ANTHONY: No. I did.

ENZO: You did not.

ANTHONY: Ask Lucy. She was watching from the window. As usual.

NAT: Lucy?

CRISTINA: Their neighbour.

ENZO: That stuck up bitch always thought she was better than us. Always calling the cops on us.

ANTHONY: Does she still live next door?

ENZO: What do you think? As if that shut-in maniac would ever leave us in peace.

ANTHONY: She called the cops on our parents the night before my bar exam. Fucking sabotaged my studying.

ENZO: Do you have your campaign posters in your car?

ANTHONY: Uh . . . yeah.

ENZO: Let's put one on her lawn!

CRISTINA: NO! Bad idea.

ANTHONY: This is not even my riding.

ENZO: Come on. Let's show her who you've become.

ANTHONY: Enzo, it is illegal to put campaign posters up without consent.

ENZO: Okay. Okay. Not her front lawn. We can dump a bunch of them in her pool.

ANTHONY: Are you joking?

> *ENZO grabs the bottle of whisky and ANTHONY's car keys off the bar and runs offstage.*

ENZO: I have your keys!

CRISTINA: Oh no.

ANTHONY: Enzo! Stop!

ANTHONY runs after him.

CRISTINA: I should probably try to stop this.

She stares at NAT for a beat.

But I'm starving all of a sudden.

NAT: Good for you. Have some gluten.

CRISTINA picks up one of the pastries.

CHRISTINE QUINTANA,
TRANSLATED BY GILLES POULIN-DENIS
SELFIE / SELFIE

Born in Los Angeles to a Mexican American father and a Dutch
British Canadian mother, Christine Quintana is now a grateful visitor
on the unceded territories of the Musqueam, Squamish, and Tsleil-
Waututh nations. Other playwriting highlights include *Never The Last*
(co-created with Molly MacKinnon), winner of a Significant Artistic
Achievement Award. Christine is a Siminovitch Prize Protégé winner
for playwriting and is currently playwright-in-residence at Tarragon
Theatre. She is a proud founding member of the Canadian Latinx
Theatre Artist Coalition and holds a B.F.A. in Acting from UBC.

Originally from Saskatoon, Gilles Poulin-Denis is an actor, playwright, director, translator, and dramaturg. His first full-length play,
Rearview, is published by Dramaturges Éditeurs and was a finalist for
the 2010 Governor General's Literary Award. It was presented in both
French and English in the fall of 2016. Gilles's second play, *Status Quo*,
was awarded the Sydney J. Risk Prize in 2013 and was finalist for the
Prix SACD de la dramaturgie francophone in 2014. It was produced
by Théâtre la Seizième in 2013 and toured throughout Canada. Wajdi
Mouawad named Gilles as one of the resident playwrights at the
National Arts Centre's Théâtre français, where he developed his play
Dehors, published by L'instant scène and presented at Theatre d'Aujo-
urd'hui and the NAC's French theatre in 2017. In 2016, Gilles co-wrote

the play *Straight Jacket Winter* with Esther Duquette, which toured Canada from 2016 to 2019 and is published by Playwrights Canada Press.

On the first day back to school, everything seems the same for Lily (Lili), her friend Emma, and her soccer-star brother Chris. They are getting ready for another year where Lily and Chris share the spotlight and Emma takes on the supporting role. Another year which will go by without Emma and Chris admitting to the feelings they have for each other. But nothing lasts forever. One wild party, one drink too many, and a camera phone are all you need to tip the scales. Propelled and reproduced by social media, a photo of Emma and Chris is being tried in the court of public opinion, and Lily must choose to either stand with her brother or her best friend—but what is truly right? Incisive and witty, *Selfie* is a powerful reflexion on sexual consent and self-promotion in this era of Instagram.

Selfie was first produced in French by Théâtre la Seizième for a school tour of Quebec in March of 2015. It was first produced in English by Young People's Theatre, Toronto, on April 26, 2018.

* * *

LILY: It's amazing

CHRIS: Fifty of Lily's girlfriends have showed up wearing sundresses

LILY: We put on sunscreen so we smell like the beach

CHRIS: And then Tyler brings out a 40 of vodka

LILY: Shot!

CHRIS: And off we go

LILY: Woo!

CHRIS: (*to LILY*) If we get busted it's all on you, okay?

LILY: No way, if the po' come I'm sending them right to you. Because you're the *favourite*, right?

CHRIS: You're the worst

LILY: Emma's missing it!

CHRIS: Why is it so hot?

LILY: (*to audience*) I turn up the heat so it feels like it's still hot outside

EMMA: (*to audience*) I open the door and it's a wall of heat and noise and bare skin

LILY: Ohmygod EMMA!

CHRIS: (*to audience*) There's gotta be a hundred people here now

LILY: You're a freakin BABE, now take a shot with me

EMMA: I think I'm good for now—

LILY: Are we doing this, or are we doing this?

> *EMMA considers for a moment, and then they take the shot.*
> *LILY turns to CHRIS.*

Chris, it's a party. Parties are fun. There are a billion people here. It's gonna be awesome. People will still like you even if we run out of ice

CHRIS: You're the worst

LILY: And yet also the best!

CHRIS: Let's do this

He takes a shot.

CHRIS: Yeeah!

EMMA: (*to audience*) And there he is

LILY: (*to audience*) "Party Chris"

CHRIS: Yo, Damien!

EMMA: (*to audience*) I can tell he's worried about impressing people, but no matter how he's feeling, Chris can always put on a smile

LILY: (*to audience*) And suddenly he's hosting this party

CHRIS: Turn it up!

LILY: (*to audience*) See?

CHRIS: What's up bruuuuuuh?

LILY: SHUTUPSHUTUP Maya is actually wearing a bikini

EMMA: (*to audience*) It's amazing

LILY: YAAAAAS

She takes a picture of the two of them. The music gets louder.

EMMA: *(to audience)* The guys from Chris's team are loving it

LILY: OH MY GOD I LOVE THIS SONG

EMMA: *(to audience)* The girls are dancing in the living room. Every window in the house is fogged up

LILY: *(to audience)* I'm sweating

CHRIS: *(to audience)* They're sweating

EMMA: *(to audience)* Everybody's sweating

LILY: I LOVE IT

EMMA: *(to audience)* I go to the kitchen

CHRIS: Ha ha, somebody actually brought a pineapple!

LILY: *(to audience)* Emma looks SUPER hot

EMMA: *(to audience)* Lily is already wasted

LILY: Look at your hair!

EMMA: *(to audience)* But every guy is looking at her

CHRIS: Gross, guys, cut that shit out!

LILY: Shot!

EMMA: (*to audience*) And I think—I'm here. He's here. This time things are going to be different

CHRIS: Hey, Emma

EMMA: It's uh, so . . . hot

CHRIS: Yeah it's . . . hot

   Awkward beat.

LILY: WowKgottagobye!

   Blackout, music stops.

EMMA: (*to audience*) And all of a sudden—

LILY: I hit the lights.

(*to party*) SHHH!

EMMA: (*to audience*) Everyone is quiet

CHRIS: Is someone at the door?

LILY: (*to audience*) There's no one at the door

EMMA: (*to audience*) Chris is beside me

CHRIS: (*to audience*) Emma is right beside me

EMMA: (*to audience*) My arm brushes his

CHRIS: (*to audience*) She's right there

EMMA: (*to audience*) And he just grabs my hand

CHRIS: (*to audience*) It's dark, and everyone is quiet

EMMA: (*to audience*) Girls are giggling

CHRIS: (*to audience*) And we're just here

EMMA: (*to audience*) Together

CHRIS: (*to* EMMA) Hey

EMMA: (*to* CHRIS) Oh hey

CHRIS: (*to* EMMA) Having fun?

LILY: (*to audience*) And then they kiss?

CHRIS *leans into* EMMA *but she awkwardly blurts:*

EMMA: (*to* CHRIS) Are you having fun?

CHRIS: (*to* EMMA) I just asked you that

EMMA: (*to* CHRIS) Sorry

LILY: (*to audience*) Dammit, Emma

(*to party*) FALSE ALARM. Shut the windows, bitches!

The music starts again, louder than before. Pictures flash on the screen behind them, blurrier and more random than before.

CHRIS: (*to audience*) The party starts again

EMMA: (*to audience*) It gets hotter and hotter

CHRIS: (*to audience*) The guys are taking off their shirts

LILY: SELFIE!

LILY pulls CHRIS and EMMA in for a selfie.

CHRIS: (*to audience*) I've never seen everyone this drunk before

EMMA: (*to audience*) I can't talk to him

CHRIS: (*to audience*) I don't think *I've* been this drunk / before, but—

LILY: / SHOTS!

EMMA, LILY, and CHRIS do shots.

EMMA: Ugh, I need water

CHRIS: (*to audience*) I should probably lock my parents' bedroom— naaaasty, there's already someone in there

LILY: OMIGOD YOU'RE KIDDING ME

CHRIS: (*to audience*) It's getting intense in here

EMMA: (*to audience*) I stumble to the bathroom to catch my breath

LILY: EMMA

> EMMA *enters the bathroom and the music and shouting grow quiet.*
> *She takes a breath. The pictures on the screen become blurrier.*

Emma, I'M COMING IN

EMMA: Wait I'm—

LILY: I need to pee

> LILY *enters the washroom.*

What's wrong?

EMMA: Just give me a second, okay, I feel like I'm gonna puke—

LILY: NOPE, NOPE. You're weening out

EMMA: No, I'm not. It's just— I don't even know how to describe it, it's like I try to say things and I just choke and I'm just saying stupid nothing words like an idiot and I wonder if it's better if I don't even try. I just wanna go home—

LILY: Stop! I know what you're trying to do, and I don't want to hear you say that. Okay? That's enough. Because you are talking about my favourite person in the whole world

EMMA: You?

LILY: No, you bitch, I'm talking about you. It makes me sad to hear you say that. It makes me *sad* to hear you say that okay? I love you

EMMA: I love you too / Lily

LILY: Like—okay, I just—I'm really nervous, okay? Like I don't want anything to change between us because you like went to Paris and found yourself and shit, and I just wanted to throw you this bigass amazing party so you don't forget bout me—

EMMA: Lily, I'd never forget about you

LILY: I just saw these pics of you at the Eiffel Tower and stuff and I was like wow, we're growing up and shit is changing and maybe we're not going to be friends forever and I like freaked the fuck out, you know? Cause like, you're my *person*. I don't want to be creepy and I don't even know why I'm so—

EMMA: You're my person too, Lily. You don't need to be worried. I'm not going anywhere. I'm just figuring myself out right now

LILY: I know. I know. OKAY REAL TALK, shake it off. Come here. Look. Your hair is large and amazing, your boobs look awesommmmeeee in that dress, and you smell like a fancy drink from Milestones. You are amazing. And I'm not the only one who thinks so. Go talk to Chris, okay? Tonight is the night. You're the two best people I know, and you're running out of time because he's gonna go away, and—okay I am like totally not crying in the bathroom because that's like literally a cliché. But go get what you deserve

She opens the door.

You know what to do

LILY leaves the bathroom. EMMA stands, staring at herself in the mirror. CHRIS stands, looking at himself in the mirror in his

room. *Party sounds remain muffled from the other side of the door. They each take a breath, and then move. Simultaneously,* CHRIS *and* EMMA *open their doors, facing each other in the hallway.*

EMMA: (*to* CHRIS) Hi

CHRIS: (*to* EMMA) Hi—are you all right?

EMMA: Yeah, it's just super hot out there, and the first day back and everything and—

CHRIS: It's a lot, yeah. I know the feeling

They share a smile.

* * *

LILI: C'est incroyable.

CHRIS: Une cinquantaine d'amies de Lili se pointe en robe d'été.

LILI: On se met de l'écran solaire, pour qu'on sente comme la plage.

CHRIS: Pis là Tyler sort un 40 onces de vodka.

LILI: Shooter!

CHRIS: Et pis ça part.

LILI: Woo!

CHRIS: (*à* LILI) Si on se fait poigner, c'est de ta faute, OK?

LILI: No way. Si les coches débarquent, c'est toi qui les gères. Parce que c'est toi le chouchou, right?

CHRIS: T'es terrible.

LILI: Emma va tout manquer!

CHRIS: Pourquoi est-ce qu'y fait tellement chaud?

LILI: (*au public*) J'ai monté le chauffage pour que ça fasse plus été.

EMMA: (*au public*) J'ouvre la porte, c'est comme un mur de chaleur pis de bruit pis de peau.

LILI: Ohmygod, Emma!

CHRIS: Y doit avoir au moins 100 personnes ici d'dans.

LILI: T'es vraiment *hot*. OK on fait des shots.

EMMA: Je pense que je suis correct pour l'instant.

LILI: T'es game ou t'es pas game?

> *EMMA hésite un instant, elles prennent un shooter. LILI se tourne vers CHRIS.*

Chris, c'est un party. C'est le fun. Y a un million de personnes ici. Ça va être malade. Le monde va continuer de t'aimer même si on manque de glaces.

CHRIS: T'es terrible.

LILI: Pis en même temps, je suis la best!

CHRIS: OK, on *start* ça.

Il prend un shooter aussi.

CHRIS: Yeeah!

EMMA: (*au public*) Mesdames et messieurs, je vous présente:

LILI: « Party CHRIS. »

CHRIS: Yo, Damien!

EMMA: (*au public*) En ce moment, il est stressé parce qu'il veut impressionner le monde. Mais peu importe comment il se sent en dedans, Chris garde toujours le sourire.

LILI: (*au public*) Et pis tout d'un coup, c'est lui qui lead le party.

CHRIS: Monte le son!

LILI: (*au public*) Vous voyez.

CHRIS: *Wassup* mon *boy*!

LILI: No way, Maya porte un bikini!

EMMA: C'est fou.

LILI: YAAAAAAS.

Elle prend une photo d'elle et EMMA. La musique monte en volume.

EMMA: (*au public*) Les gars de l'équipe à Chris adorent ça.

LILI: OH MY GOD J'ADORE CETTE CHANSON.

EMMA: (*au public*) Les filles dansent dans le salon. Toutes les fenêtres sont embuées.

LILI: (*au public*) Je sue.

CHRIS: (*au public*) Ils suent.

EMMA: (*au public*) Tout le monde sue.

LILI: J'ADORE ÇA.

EMMA: (*au public*) Je m'en vais à la cuisine.

CHRIS: Ha ha, quelqu'un a apporté un ananas!

LILI: (*au public*) Emma est vraiment *chix*.

EMMA: (*au public*) Lili est déjà saoule.

LILI: *Check* tes cheveux!

EMMA: (*au public*) Mais tous les gars regardent Lili.

CHRIS: Guys, arrêtez ça, c'est *gross*.

LILI: Shooter!

EMMA: (*au public*) Mais moi je me dis—je suis là. Lui, y est là. Cette fois-ci ça sera pas pareil.

CHRIS: Hey, Emma.

EMMA: Y fait tellement, euh . . . chaud.

CHRIS: Oui, y fait . . . chaud.

Malaise.

LILI: WowOKfautquej'yaillebye.

Blackout, la musique cesse.

EMMA: (*au public*) Pis tout d'un coup.

LILI: J'éteins les lumières.

(*au party*) SHHH!

EMMA: (*au public*) Tout le monde est silencieux.

CHRIS: Est-ce qu'y a quelqu'un à la porte?

LILI: (*au public*) Il y a personne à la porte.

EMMA: (*au public*) Chris est à côté de moi.

CHRIS: (*au public*) Emma est juste à côté de moi.

EMMA: (*au public*) Mon bras frôle le sien.

CHRIS: (*au public*) Elle est juste là.

EMMA: (*au public*) Pis y fait juste prendre ma main.

CHRIS: (*au public*) Il fait noir, tout le monde est silencieux.

EMMA: (*au public*) Y a des filles qui rient.

CHRIS: (*au public*) Et pis on est juste là.

EMMA: (*au public*) Ensemble.

CHRIS: (*à EMMA*) Hey.

EMMA: (*à CHRIS*) Oh, hey.

CHRIS: (*à EMMA*) Tu t'amuses?

LILI: (*au public*) Et pis là, ils s'embrassent?

> *CHRIS s'avance vers EMMA, mais elle répond maladroitement:*

EMMA: (*à CHRIS*) Est-ce que tu t'amuses?

CHRIS: (*à EMMA*) J'viens juste de te demander ça.

EMMA: (*à CHRIS*) Oh, 'scuse.

LILI: (*au public*) Shit, EMMA.

(*au party*) Fausse alarme! Fermez les fenêtres, bitchezzz!

> *La musique recommence, plus forte qu'auparavant. Des photos flashent sur l'écran derrière, de plus en plus flou.*

CHRIS: (*au public*) Le party repart.

EMMA: (*au public*) Y fait de plus en plus chaud.

CHRIS: (*au public*) Les gars enlèvent leur chandail.

LILI: SELFIE!

> *LILI attrape* CHRIS *et* EMMA *et prend une photo.*

CHRIS: (*au public*) J'ai jamais vu le monde aussi saoul.

EMMA: (*au public*) Je peux pas lui parler.

CHRIS: (*au public*) J'pense pas que moi, j'ai jamais été aussi saoul/ avant, mais—

LILI: / SHOOTER!

> EMMA, LILI, *et* CHRIS *prennent un shooter.*

EMMA: Ugh, j'ai besoin d'un verre d'eau.

CHRIS: (*au public*) Je devrais probablement barrer la chambre de mes parents— Ewww, il y a déjà du monde là-dedans.

LILI: OHMYGOD TU ME NIAISES.

CHRIS: (*au public*) Ça commence à être pas mal intense là.

EMMA: (*au public*) Je plonge dans la salle de bain pour reprendre mon souffle.

LILI: Emma.

EMMA entre dans la salle de bain, la musique et les cris diminuent. Elle respire un peu. Les photos sur l'écran sont de plus en plus floues.

EMMA, JE RENTRE.

EMMA: Attends, je suis—

LILI: Faut que je pisse.

LILI entre dans la salle de bain.

Qu'est-ce qu'il y a?

EMMA: Donne-moi une minute OK, on dirait que je vais vomir—

LILI: NON. NON. T'es en train de choker.

EMMA: Non, c'est pas vrai. C'est juste—je sais pas comment dire, c'est comme si j'essaie de parler pis je bloque, je fais juste dire des choses vides pis stupides comme une conne, pis je me dis que c'est peut-être mieux si j'arrête d'essayer. Je veux juste rentrer—

LILI: Wo! Je sais ce que t'essaies de faire, pis je veux pas t'entendre dire ces choses-là, OK? C'est assez. Tu parles pas de même de la personne que j'aime le plus au monde.

EMMA: Qui? Toi?

LILI: T'es conne. Non, je parle de toi. Ça me fait de la peine que tu dises ça. Ça me fait de la peine, OK? Je t'aime.

EMMA: Je t'aime aussi / Lili.

LILI: Parce que—c'est juste—je suis stressé, OK? Je veux pas que les choses changent entre nous parce que t'es allée à Paris pis que t'as vécu de quoi pis c'te shit-là. Je voulais juste organiser un gros party de fou pour pas que tu m'oublies—

EMMA: Lili, je vais jamais t'oublier.

LILI: C'est juste que j'ai vu les photos de toi devant la tour Eiffel pis j'étais comme : Wow, on est en train de grandir pis toute change et peut-être qu'on va pas être amie pour toujours pis j'ai fuckin' freaké, tsé? Parce que t'es comme mon âme soeur. Je veux pas sonner creepy pis je sais même pas pourquoi je suis tellement—

EMMA: Toi aussi, t'es mon âme soeur, Lili. Fais-toi s'en pas. Je m'en vais pas là. Je suis juste en train de gérer mes affaires ces temps-ci.

LILI: Je sais. Je sais. OK, pour vrai. Viens ici. Check. Tes cheveux sont gros pis magnifiques, tes seins ont l'air juste sublime dans ta robe, tu sens comme un drink sucré de chez Milestones. T'es magnifique, tout le monde le pense. Là, va parler à Chris, OK? C'est ce soir que ça se passe. Vous êtes les meilleures personnes au monde, pis il reste pas beaucoup de temps, parce qu'après il va partir, pis—OK, je vais tellement pas pleurer dans la salle de bain parce que ça, c'est juste trop cliché. (*Elle ouvre la porte.*) Tu sais quoi faire.

> *LILI quitte la salle de bain. EMMA demeure seule, face au miroir. CHRIS est dans sa chambre, également debout face à un miroir. Le bruit provenant de la fête est en sourdine. Ils prennent tous deux une grande inspiration. EMMA et CHRIS ouvrent leur porte au même instant, se retrouvant face à face dans le couloir.*

EMMA: (*à CHRIS*) Allo

CHRIS: (*à* EMMA) *Allo. Ça va?*

EMMA: *Ouais. C'est juste qu'il fait super chaud, pis je viens juste de revenir en ville et puis . . .*

CHRIS: *Ouais, c'est intense. Je sais ce que c'est.*

Ils se sourient.

EVAN TSITSIAS
AFTERSHOCK

Evan's plays include *Aftershock* (Tom Hendry Nomination for Best
New Comedy, Best of SummerWorks), *The Murmuration of Starlings*
(Honourable Mention in the Herman Voaden National Playwriting
Competition), *Unstuck* (Frank Theatre Company), and *Strange Mary
Strange* (Best of SummerWorks). His short film BAGGED aired on
CBC Television, the National Screen Institute, and at the DC Shorts
International Film Festival. He co-created/co-wrote/co-directed *I am
Invisible*, *Berlin Bound*, and *We Are the Play* in Germany, ECHO in Greece,
and has directed in Italy. In Taiwan, he co-created the play *In Transit*.
He's also directed and created work in New York City, Houston, and
around Canada. He is a member of the Tarragon Playwrights Unit and
has been nominated for the Dora Mavor Moore Award, Broadwayworld
Awards, the John Hirsch Director's Award, and has been a finalist
for the Charles Abbott Directing Fellowship. He is Artistic Director/
Co-Founder of the Directors Lab North, co-founder of the World Wide
Lab, and member of the Lincoln Center and Chicago Directors Lab. He's
spent several years at Theatre Under the Stars and on the faculty of the
Humphreys School of Musical Theatre in Houston. He is the founding
and former artistic director of Eclipse Theatre Company in Toronto. His
book, *The Directors Lab*, was published by Playwrights Canada Press in
2019. For more information, visit www.evantsitsias.com.

First you revere it, then you want to destroy it. Anna returns to her
mobile park home after appearing in an "extreme plastic surgery
makeover" show on television. Her radical transformation ignites a

sea of change, wreaking havoc on her eccentric family and town, who seem to have all lost the ability to communicate with Anna and her exquisite beauty. Anna must now take drastic measures to either fully inhabit her new persona or demolish it completely in order to survive.

Aftershock was first produced at the Factory Studio Theatre as part of the SummerWorks Festival, Toronto, on August 10, 2010.

* * *

In black, the sounds of renovation are heard.

A saw hacks away.

A hammer hits a nail hard.

An electric drill spins fast.

The sounds crescendo into a symphony of renovation. Something grand is being built. As the sounds climax they suddenly stop.

Nothing.

Lights snap up to reveal ANNA standing centre stage in the interior of a trailer home. It's tacky, trashy, terrible, typical. Not one matching item in sight. But ANNA is beautiful. Perfect. She is dressed all in white. Sparkling head to toe. A china doll in a dumpster. She is surrounded by GARY, MOM, QUINN, and BECKY. They all smile at her. And stare. No one says a word. For an uncomfortably long time. Finally . . .

ANNA: Say something.

An explosion of reactions:

MOM: Well honey, you just look so darn fancy, I need to come up with something fancy to say t'ya.

BECKY: You look so . . . different.

GARY: Like an angel.

MOM: That's it! One of those angels you see in church. All shiny and shit.

GARY: She's perfect.

General agreement. The following dialogue is all overlapping.

MOM: You've changed, Annabel.

BECKY: Transformed.

GARY: Annabel?

MOM: That's her real name. There was no need to call her that.

Till now.

BECKY: Did they fill in that gap in your teeth?

MOM: They sure are white.

BECKY: What did they do to them?

GARY: Perfect.

MOM: I'd eat a pound of horseshit for teeth that white.

BECKY: Veneers?

MOM: That little paint bottle thingy?

BECKY: And look at your nose.

GARY: Perfect.

BECKY: So small.

MOM: Bleach?

BECKY: And straight.

MOM: Those strip watchamacallits?

GARY: Like an angel.

MOM: Or that thingamajig? / Aw shit—with the light . . .

BECKY: Your nostrils are so tiny.

MOM: That blue light thingamabob . . .

BECKY: My nose looks like a cashew.

MOM: Laser! That's it. Shit.

BECKY: Or a pecan.

MOM: They look like diamonds.

BECKY: Your nose used to look like a banana.

GARY: Perfect.

BECKY: They called you Anna Banana.

MOM: You look like such a lady.

BECKY: Remember? /

GARY: Amazing. /

BECKY: (*chanting it like the kids used to*) "Anna Banana."

MOM: Like a teenager again.

BECKY: She never looked like that!

GARY: Perfect.

BECKY: (*chanting again*) Anna Banana. Remember?!

GARY: Just perfect.

BECKY: And your hair.

MOM: If I had teeth like that things would have been different.

BECKY: Are they extensions?

GARY: Like an angel.

MOM: I would have been . . . !

MOM *makes a rocket launching noise.*

BECKY: Mine's all wirey.

GARY: My angel.

BECKY: Is it a special conditioner?

MOM: I'm telling ya I'da been . . .

MOM *makes an explosion noise.*

GARY: That's what you are.

BECKY: Maybe I can order it online.

MOM: Oh ya Becky can use some of that.

BECKY: (*to* MOM) I can?

GARY: Beautiful.

MOM: (*to* BECKY) Your hair's as dry as a pile of hay in the desert.

BECKY: Mother!

MOM: I'm just trying to help.

GARY: Your dress is beautiful.

MOM: Forget the dress, look at those tits!

BECKY: They're implants.

GARY: Perfect.

BECKY: Augmented, right?

MOM: Isn't that a fancy word for big boobs?

BECKY: I could never pull that off.

GARY: An angel.

MOM: Becky's tits are like bee stings.

BECKY: Mother.

MOM: All nipple.

BECKY: Mother, please!

MOM: You're a late bloomer.

BECKY: I don't appreciate it when you criticize me like that.

MOM: Oh put it in neutral, Becky.

BECKY: It's just difficult to be constantly bombarded with negativity.

MOM: Don't you start that Oprah shit.

BECKY: I'm feeling very fragile right now and I'd appreciate some positive affirmation.

MOM: Don't be stupid.

GARY: Look at my angel.

BECKY: Everyone's fawning over Anna and no one is honouring my . . . authentic spirit.

MOM: You don't even know what that means, Becky.

BECKY: REBECCA!

MOM: Have some friggin' respect, there's a lady present, stupid.

BECKY: I'm an adult mother. I will not be spoken to like that.

MOM: Then quitch'er whining. You did the same thing when you were little. "Na na na wah wah wah. Feed me, hug me, love me." What a baby!

BECKY: I WAS A BABY!

MOM: Always an excuse. Jesus H. Christ! Sorry, Annabel.

BECKY: I'd really appreciate if you called me by my full name as well.

MOM: And I'd "appreciate" if you shut your pie hole for a minute.

BECKY: My real name is Rebecca.

MOM: I named you, stupid!

GARY: It's just . . .

BECKY: Oh god I can't breathe.

MOM: Back up, folks, Becky's gonna blow!

GARY: You're an angel!

BECKY: (*trying to catch her breath*) RE-BE-CCA.

BECKY inhales deeply.

GARY: My angel.

MOM: Stop that, Becky.

BECKY: REBECCA!

GARY: My Annabel.

BECKY: REBECCA REBECCA REBECCA!

BECKY passes out. They all stop. After several moments MOM bursts out laughing. ANNA takes a step to help BECKY up but—

GARY/MOM: NO!!

ANNA freezes . . . one foot in front of her.

MOM: What are you doing?

GARY: You're so beautiful right there.

ANNA looks at BECKY.

MOM: Just leave 'er. You're not supposed to move 'er. It "confuses" 'em. Shit.

ANNA slowly takes her foot back and stands back in place. GARY and MOM exhale.

GARY: Perfect.

MOM: Don't worry, the doctor says just leave 'er so I leave 'er. She'll be fine. She's just playing around anyway. AREN'T YA, BECKY!!

She lifts up BECKY's arm then lets go. It flops hard on the floor.

See. At least now we got some peace and quiet. So we can sit here and just lookatcha.

GARY: Another few minutes. For us.

GARY sits.

MOM: Don't you move, Annabel.

MOM sits.

GARY: Just stay right there.

MOM: Your teeth are so damn white.

GARY: You're just . . . beautiful.

MOM: Pound of horseshit, I'm telling ya.

ANNA just . . . stands there. BECKY is still passed out. MOM and GARY just stare, smiling. So ANNA does too. QUINN does not. They all stay there. For a long time.

COLLEEN MURPHY
I HOPE MY HEART BURNS FIRST

Colleen Murphy's plays *Pig Girl* and *The December Man / L'homme de décembre* won the Governor General's Literary Award for Drama and the Carol Bolt Award. Other plays include *The Society For The Destitute Presents Titus Bouffonius, The Breathing Hole, Armstrong's War, The Goodnight Bird, Beating Heart Cadaver, The Piper, Down in Adoration Falling,* and *All Other Destinations are Cancelled.* Twice she won awards in the CBC Literary Competition for *Fire-Engine Red* and *Pumpkin Eaters.* Libretti include *Oksana G.*, composed by Aaron Gervais, and *My Mouth On Your Heart*, composed by August Murphy-King. Her distinct, award-winning films have played in festivals around the world. Colleen has been the playwright- and writer-in-residence at a number of theatres and universities, most recently, Writer in Residence at the University of New Brunswick.

When a group of young people break into a mansion to steal stuff to pay off a drug debt, they unexpectedly confront their own ambition and sense of futility. Full of dark comedy and wild abandon, *I Hope My Heart Burns First* dramatizes the emotional cost of economic disparity to reveal the bottomless rage that often fuels the working poor.

I Hope My Heart Burns First premiered at the Timms Centre at the University of Alberta's Department of Drama, Edmonton, on March 20, 2017, under the title *Bright Burning*.

* * *

Enter FLEUR *followed by* LARKIN *and* J. *They are dressed some-
what like the others who are already inside, but their clothes are
a bit sharper.*

DEON: Hey, Fleur—how'd you get in?

FLEUR: Side door's wide open.

DEON: That's to welcome you.

FLEUR: (*looking around*) Awesome. I didn't know you came from
wealth like this . . .

LARKIN: Lookit—flowers—lookit the colours all the colours in the
world.

*LARKIN puts her arms around the flowers in the big vase and liter-
ally lifts them all out and hugs them close.*

J: (*to* DEON) Hey, bro . . .

J makes a swift beeline for DEON *and grabs him by the neck . . .*

. . . you're dead you're so fucking dead I'm gonna kill you five more
times—

DEON: I know I owe her but I'm paying—

. . . and shoves DEON *up hard against the closest available wall.*

ow, Fleur, you need to keep buddy on a tight leash—

FLEUR: Buddy's name is J—

DEON: Yeah I know J—you need to keep—

FLEUR: J's for Jarvis a Teutonic name that means spear servant. He's a Virgo ruled by Mercury the god of travellers an' guide of souls to the underworld.

DEON: Okay, Jarvis—

FLEUR: No, fuckface, you do not get to call him by his real name.

DEON: Okay sorry—J.

FLEUR: Let him go, Jarvis.

J steps back from DEON.

JOCELYN: (*to* FLEUR) I'm fiending for some shabu.

LOU: Yeah, Fleur, I jus need a little bit to fuck me up enough to feel normal.

FLEUR: What's with the rubber gloves and shit—your dad have some contagious disease or something.

Silence.

LOU: . . . yeah Deon's dad had . . . Ebola.

FLEUR: What's that—like measles?

EMILY: (*closes her eyes*) "Ebola is a viral hemorrhagic fever of human and other primates cause by ebolaviruses and carried a high risk of death with—"

FLEUR: Fuck this.

(to LARKIN and J) We're outta here—

DEON: Hold it wait this isn't my dad's house.

JOCELYN: Yeah it is, it's his dead dad's house.

DEON: No it's not—

JOCELYN: Yeah you told us to say it—

LOU: *(to JOCELYN)* Shut up.

DEON: *(to FLEUR)* It belongs to someone I know but they're in Hawaii . . . I made up that story about my dad in order to get you here.

FLEUR: I knew something stank.

(to J) Kill him.

J: You're so dead—

DEON: No wait—

> *J grabs DEON by the neck, pushes him on the floor, and yanks him backward by the neck as DEON struggles.*

LOU: IT'S HIS DAD'S HOUSE, ASSHOLE—

JOCELYN: YEAH HIS DAD'S HOUSE—HIS DEAD DAD'S HOUSE—

FLEUR: J, enough.

J lets DEON *go.*

Whose fucking house is this, Deon—

DEON: . . . yeah okay it belongs to my dad . . . he didn't have Ebola or anything . . . I just don't want the rest of my family to know we're stripping the place tonight so yeah cover your face because of surveillance and put on gloves then take whatever you want as payback.

J: Be right back.

J exits, pulling a knife out of his coat.

DEON: Where's he—

FLEUR: I think you're fucking lying.

DEON: It's true, Fleur, he's dead.

LOU: Yeah dead forever.

DEON: Like I hated him even though I loved him.

FLEUR: Scorpios are s'posed to be emotional—maybe in secret, Deon, maybe in the dead dark snake pit of your inner life—lemme see your hand.

DEON pulls off a glove and offers her his right hand—she looks at his palm.

JOCELYN: Fleur, I'm fiending bad.

FLEUR: You an' the rest of the world, hon.

(*to* DEON *about his hand*) Your heart line's short an' your life line is long.

DEON: I'm going to live to be a hundred.

FLEUR: Unless you're lying eh then you'll only live a few more minutes.

DEON: My dad's dead, Fleur.

LARKIN: Lying is lying.

FLEUR: Yeah, hon, lying is lying.

DEON: I'm not lying. No it was a massive heart attack dead before he hit the floor, so just take whatever you want—jewellery, art, shit, clothes, whatever—

FLEUR: I could use a new bedroom set, eh—king-size bed, nice big mattress, fancy duvet pillow shams.

DEON: C'mon, have a drink, there's lots of wine.

FLEUR: Gimme your scarf.

    FLEUR *pulls the scarf off* LARKIN's *neck.*

LARKIN: What am I s'posed to use.

FLEUR: (*indicating the flowers*) Hold those in front of your face . . .

    LARKIN *holds up the flowers.*

Okay gimme a mojito.

DEON: Ari—drinks all around.

JOCELYN offers FLEUR one of the candelabra.

JOCELYN: I need something now eh—

LOU offers the box of gloves to FLEUR.

LOU: They're real surgery gloves—sanitized even.

ARI: What's a mojito.

FLEUR: White rum, six leaves of mint, soda water, lime juice, and sugar.

ARI: Mint eh.

J enters.

J: I cut everything inside an' outside.

FLEUR: Thanks, hon.

(to everyone else) You can take the shit off your faces now.

(to LOU) Gimme a coupla pair of those gloves. Larkin an' J, put on a pair of these.

ARI: Not sure where to find mint.

LOU: Fleur, I'm fiending so bad I tried to commit suicide jus now.

JOCELYN: *(referring to the chandelier)* Yeah she did from right up there eh 'cuz we need some shit like instantly.

LOU: (*to FLEUR*) Yeah you take this an'...

LOU grabs the candelabra from JOCELYN.

Here...

FLEUR: I'd never commit suicide 'cuz I don't wanna come back as a raccoon or drug addict.

LOU: Here.

LOU tries to give the candelabra to FLEUR.

I'm paying you in advance.

DEON takes the candelabra from LOU, but LOU grabs it back from him.

DEON: What'll you have to drink, J.

J: Triple vodka on the rocks.

FLEUR: This place is fucking magnificent—your dad got a safe we can smash?

DEON: Probably—but I don't know where he kept it.

FLEUR: J, go find it.

J exits upstairs.

DEON: Larkin—want a drink?

FLEUR: Give her a Moscow mule.

ARI: How you make that?

LARKIN touches JOCELYN's coat.

LARKIN: This real fur?

FLEUR: (*to LARKIN*) Don't you go touching anything till you put on a pair of these.

ARI: How you make a mule?

JOCELYN: Yeah, mink. Pretty gorgeous, eh.

LARKIN: I can't bear that animals are suffering an' being skinned.

LOU: Me neither. I'm gonna be a vet.

JOCELYN: This one isn't suffering, it's already dead.

ARI: (*to LOU*) You ever heard of that mule drink?

FLEUR: Smirnoff, ginger beer, an' fresh lime juice.

ARI exits.

JOCELYN: (*to FLEUR*) I love you unequivocally.

FLEUR: Unequivocally, eh.

JOCELYN: Yeah—that's one of Lou's words she learned in jail.

LOU: It's not my word, asshole—anyone can use it.

JOCELYN takes her fur off and drapes it over FLEUR.

FLEUR: (*to DEON*) You owe me two thousand four hundred an' sixty-five dollars.

DEON: Wow shit . . . that much.

FLEUR: That's too much.

LARKIN: (*looking at EMILY's hiked up dress*) Like why's your dress like that.

FLEUR: Two thousand four hundred an' sixty-five dollars is jus too much eh.

DEON: Yeah . . . it got away on me.

EMILY: I'm going to swing from the chandelier.

FLEUR: I think you were trying to get away from me.

DEON: No—I just didn't have the money.

LARKIN: I wanna chance too.

EMILY: I'm next in line. You could be after me. Stand behind me.

LARKIN does so.

FLEUR: (*to DEON*) Say that number out loud to my face.

EMILY: ARI, COULD YOU SPOT US?

DEON: Two thousand four hundred and sixty-five I was going to pay you, Fleur. I had it, then spent it, but I got it now.

JOCELYN tries to put a piece of jewellery on FLEUR.

FLEUR: *(to JOCELYN)* Okay thank you go away.

(to DEON) Gimme the money.

DEON: I don't have it in cash yet but there's a shitload of expensive stuff in this place, Fleur—just reach out and take it.

FLEUR: It's hot.

DEON: Yeah for five minutes, then it's yours to sell, melt down, dismantle, or take it over to Puff—you'll come out a rich woman.

FLEUR: I don't deal with that fuck—he's a snitch.

DEON: Take it to whomever you want—take everything just take and take and take—

FLEUR: YOU'RE THE BITCH OWES ME, YOU GET THAT—YOU OWE ME—

DEON: Yeah I know but—

FLEUR: You pick out the shit from here, you take it down to Puff, you get the cash, then you hand me the cash—J will accompany you.

JOCELYN: Please, Fleur, please—

FLEUR: Fuck off—no one's getting anything until that money's in my hand—

DEON: It's a deal.

FLEUR: Where's my drink.

DEON: (*calls*) ARI.

J enters.

J: No safe—can't find a safe.

FLEUR: There's always a safe—keep looking.

JOCELYN: (*to FLEUR*) You like perfume—here's Joy JEAN PA-TOU.

FLEUR physically goes after JOCELYN.

FLEUR: (*to JOCELYN*) I told you you'll get something when the accounts are—

LOU: (*to FLEUR*) Hey don't beat on Joce—

JOCELYN: (*to FLEUR*) You are so cruel.

EMILY: WOULD SOMEONE PLEASE SPOT US.

FLEUR: Larkin—get down here an' put these on.

LARKIN doesn't move.

J: (*to LOU*) World Suicide Prevention Day is September 10th eh.

LOU: What's that s'posed to mean.

FLEUR: (*calls*) Larkin.

J: Suicide prevention begins with recognizing warning signs an'—

LOU: Get outta my face.

J: I know it's hard for those of you suffering to talk 'bout your feelings, but me, I've bin there—

LOU: GET THE FUCK OUTTA MY FACE!

FLEUR: JARVIS!

J: I'm trying to help her understand suicide's dangerous an'—

DEON: Lou—go grab the most expensive jewellery you can find because I need something like fucking yesterday.

LOU: Me too—I'm fiending so bad.

EMILY: Lou, Larkin and I want a turn. Would you spot us?

LOU: Later . . .

> LOU *exits upstairs.*

J: Fuck her.

FLEUR: Lou's a sensitive being an' possesses the same sensitivities you do.

J: Yeah I'm sensitive being.

FLEUR: What do you want—new watch, some boots—

J: I want my drink—I WANT MY FUCKING VODKA.

FLEUR: (*re: the gloves*) Larkin, get your ass down here an' put these on.

LARKIN: I don't want to lose my place in line.

FLEUR: Jarvis.

> *In one motion J strides up, grabs LARKIN, and yanks her down the stairs. There is a moment of startledness among the others . . . but it passes quickly.*

LARKIN: OW OW OW OW.

FLEUR: Don't bruise her.

EMILY: YOU ARE HURTING LARKIN—

FLEUR: Shut your hole.

(*to LARKIN*) Here, hon—put these on.

> *LARKIN obediently pulls on the gloves then puts the flowers in front of her face. A loud smashing sound as the upstage wall breaks against the force of a boat on a trailer hitch crashing backward into the room then coming to a halt.*

DEON: . . . what the hell . . .

FLEUR: Run.

EMILY: BOMB.

LARKIN: Help.

The sound of a truck idling, then the sound of a truck door opening.

DARNELL: (*offstage*) OH SHIT . . .

DEON: YOU FUCKING SMASHED THE WALL.

DARNELL: (*offstage*) IT WAS AN ACCIDENT—I'LL DRIVE HER BACK OUT . . .

The back of the boat and the hitch start to move out, and more of the wall falls down.

DEON: STOP STOP—YOU'RE GOING TO BUST THE WALL MORE, ASSHOLE. OH MY GOD . . .

DEON exits through a section of the hole and over the boat, then we hear the sound of a truck engine being turned off.

FUTURE

MARIE CLEMENTS
THE UNNATURAL AND ACCIDENTAL WOMEN

Marie Clements is an award-winning Métis performer, playwright, and director whose work has been presented on international stages. She is the founder of urban ink productions, a Vancouver-based First Nations production company that creates, develops, and produces Aboriginal and multicultural works of theatre, dance, music, film, and video. Clements was invited to the prestigious Festival TransAmériques for *Urban Tattoo* and *Burning Vision,* and worked in the writing department of the television series *Da Vinci's Inquest.* A fellowship award from the BC Film Commission enabled her to develop the film adaptation of *The Unnatural and Accidental Women.* She is also a regular contributor on CBC Radio. The world premiere of *Copper Thunderbird* was the first time Canada's National Arts Centre produced the work of a First Nations playwright on its main stage.

The Unnatural and Accidental Women is a surrealist dramatization of a thirty-year murder case involving many mysterious deaths in the "Skid Row" area of Vancouver. All the victims were found dead with a blood-alcohol reading far beyond safe levels, and all were last seen in the company of Gilbert Paul Jordan, who frequented the city's bars preying on primarily middle-aged Native women. The coroner's reports listed the cause of death of many of these women as "unnatural and accidental." Marie Clements reconstructs the lives of these women as shaped by lost connections—to loved ones, to the land, to a way of life—lives at times desperate, at times tender, yearning for ties of communication, belonging, and shelter gone dead. These are precariously vulnerable lives, so easily drawn to their end by the heat and light of a flame, lives that thirst for an end of searching in forgetfulness.

The Unnatural and Accidental Women premiered on November 2, 2000, and ran until November 25 at the Firehall Arts Centre in Vancouver.

* * *

GILBERT: I am a good and decent man.
I am a good and good-living man.

MAVIS, VALERIE, and VIOLET appear behind VERNA.

VALERIE places her hand on VERNA's shoulder.

VALERIE: It's time to go, Verna—he's not worth it.

GILBERT: I am clean.

MAVIS: He's just a man.

GILBERT: I am.

VERNA: An ugly man to boot.

GILBERT: I am.

VIOLET: An ugly man to boot.

GILBERT: I am.

MAVIS: You should feel sorry for him.

GILBERT: Therefore, I am.

VERNA: Sorry?

Pause.

All I feel sorry for is his little dick and his ugly face. Besides, I'm tired of feeling sorry for white people.

GILBERT continues to get blasted.

MAVIS: Okay, enough of this ugly.

VERNA: What? You got something for him, Mavis?

MAVIS: I never had anything for him, Verna. I thought he was some-one else.

VERNA: Well, that's easy to say now . . .

VALERIE: That's enough, Verna. We all thought he was someone we knew. Someone we needed. Okay, leave it alone.

VERNA: Skinny bastard.

MAVIS: We should go, Verna.

VERNA: You go.

VALERIE: We're not leaving you here, Verna.

VERNA: Why the hell not?

VALERIE: It would be too pitiful.

VERNA: You wanna make something out of this, Valerie?

VALERIE: Verna, you know I could make you in a minute.

VERNA gets up from her chair to challenge VALERIE.

VERNA: Make this . . .

MAVIS: Hello—it's her Rebecca.

VALERIE & VIOLET: Oh shitttttttttttttttttttt . . .

REBECCA approaches them. The WOMEN back away slightly.

REBECCA: Excuse me?

WOMEN: Ahhhh . . . yeah?

GILBERT: *(hazy drunk)* Yeah? What do you want?

He looks at her intensely.

I mean . . . how can I help you? Miss.

REBECCA: Umm . . . the guy at the front said you were the one that had my wallet. I mean you were the one that found it. Remember, you told me to get the bartender to point you out.

GILBERT: Right . . . right. Mind isn't what it used to be.

GILBERT laughs.

Have a seat.

REBECCA sits.

I saw you in here last night. It must of fell from your jacket or something. I'm just glad I could help.

VALERIE: Help this, you fuckin pig!

VALERIE squeezes her boobs together.

REBECCA: Well, thanks. It's always a big hassle when you lose your ID.

WOMEN: I'll say.

GILBERT: What's a nice girl like you hanging around a place like this?

MAVIS: Oh, that's original.

REBECCA: Just playing pool.

GILBERT: Can I buy you a drink?

VIOLET: No.

REBECCA: No, it's okay.

GILBERT: Seriously, you look like a lady that was lookin' for something.

He hands her over a beer. She watches the beer slide over.

REBECCA: O-kay . . . Well, it's a long story.

GILBERT: I got all the time in the world.

REBECCA: Really. I have been looking for my mother. She was last seen in this neighbourhood. Seems I just get close to where she last lived, or where she used to hang out, and I somehow miss her.

GILBERT: You gotta picture? I've been around here for a long time.

REBECCA shuffles in her purse and pulls a picture out. She shows it to him.

All the WOMEN look at it.

VALERIE: Holy shit, she was beautiful.

MAVIS: Kinda looks like me when I was young.

VERNA: Yeah, right.

GILBERT: I think I know her. I think her name was—well . . . I don't know her real name, but they used to call her Aunt Shadie or something . . .

REBECCA: Aunt Shadie?

WOMEN: Aunt Shadie?!

GILBERT: Aunt Shadie. Come to think of it, I had a drink with her awhile back.

REBECCA: How long ago is a while back?

GILBERT: I lose track of time—you know how it is? Anyways, she left some things with me to hold for safekeeping . . . she said she was gonna try and look up a daughter she hadn't seen in awhile. I'm always tryin' to help some of these women out.

REBECCA: Really.

GILBERT: If you want, we can finish these off and head over to my barbershop. I think I got something of hers there.

The GILBERT watches her as REBECCA downs her beer. They get up, and he stumbles and tries to pull himself together. REBECCA looks around, she stops.

WOMEN: It's all right.

CIARÁN MYERS
COFFEE BOMBS

Ciarán Myers holds an M.F.A. in Writing for Stage and Broadcast Media from the Royal Central School of Speech and Drama. Selected writing credits to date include *Touch* (Edinburgh Fringe), *The Adding* (Off West End), *Egon Schiele* (Almost Random Theatre, Oxford), *The House of Fun* (Green Light Arts, Kitchener, ON), *Hamburger* (Toronto Fringe), and *Creation Story* (Kitchener). Ciarán is a multi-published poet, champion Irish dancer, and proud father. He is also an alumnus of the University of Waterloo, the Traverse Theatre's Directing Program, the Tron Theatre's 100 Club, and the Stratford Festival's playwright's retreat. Selected acting credits include *Woyzeck*, *The Taming of the Shrew*, and *Mad Forest*.

The town is under attack, a young girl must choose between saving herself or her friend.

Coffee Bombs was first produced as part of a new writing showcase by M.F.A. students at the Royal Central School of Speech and Drama in London, UK, on March 15, 2014.

* * *

A coffee shop.

Enter BARISTA, *who sings to the empty room.*

From outside can be heard the voices of children:

BOY: Okay. Let's play a game.

GIRL 1: Is it a hard game?

GIRL 2: Just tell us what you see.

BOY: Except you don't actually say what you see.

GIRL 2: Sort of.

BOY: You say what it's like.

GIRL 1: Okay.

GIRL 2: I'll start. I see a rat.

The BARISTA *pours tequila into the bottom of a coffee cup. S/he leaves the bottle on the counter.*

BOY: Oh, that's a good one. I see a thumbtack sitting where I sat.

The sudden sound of bombs going off at an almost safe distance.

The BARISTA *ducks behind the counter quickly, after a beat s/he peeks back out.*

The sound continues, more distantly; lights flicker. Noticing that the barrage isn't on their doorstep s/he starts to go about their business, wiping the counter, etc. S/he downs the shot from their cup and sets out to keep working.

The three young children run into the coffee shop, tucking their heads down for the explosions. They look out the window over the audience. Although all three are clearly frightened, BOY and GIRL 2 are also excited, gleeful.

Keep playing!

GIRL 1: I see a scarecrow.

BOY: I see a nest!

GIRL 2: I see a man's hand reaching for my chest.

BARISTA: What are you doing?

GIRL 1: (*recognizing the BARISTA*) Jamie!

An explosion, nearer.

BOY: That one was a giant milkshake, spaloosh! All over!

BARISTA: Get over here!

The BOY laughs.

GIRL 1 goes to the counter; she is ushered behind it by the BARISTA.

GIRL 1 whispers something in the BARISTA's ear.

It's okay. I know.

GIRL 1: No, you don't!

BARISTA: It's okay.

> *GIRL 1 looks back up at the BARISTA, angry that they are not more attentive to her whisper.*

GIRL 2: Can I have a drink?

BARISTA: What?

GIRL 2: A cup of coffee.

BARISTA: No. Get away from the window!

> *More explosions in the distance.*

> *GIRL 1 gives the slightest little whimper; she is glad to be behind the counter with the BARISTA.*

> *GIRL 2 does a pirouette.*

BOY: I see a great wheel reeling up into the sky.

GIRL 2: We want some refreshment to accompany the show.

BARISTA: You can't have coffee.

BOY: Why not?

BARISTA: You won't like it.

GIRL 2: How do you know?

BARISTA: You're too young.

GIRL 2: You're too young!

BARISTA: I'm a . . . wo/man.

GIRL 2: A wo/man is just a girl/boy.

BOY: What does coffee taste like?

BARISTA: Like being grown up!

BOY: (*to* GIRL 1) Pour us some coffee.

She doesn't.

BARISTA: There isn't any.

BOY: Why not?

BARISTA: Because—

An explosion, very close. Lights go out entirely. Black.

Beat.

GIRL 2: (*speaking softly*) Hey, what's that one like?

BOY: I see a . . . it's like, ah . . .

GIRL 1: Like a blanket.

BOY: . . . yeah!

The lights start to flicker back on, slowly becoming steady again.

All are visible except the BARISTA.

Where's Jamie?

GIRL 1 looks down, indicating that s/he is hiding behind the counter.

BARISTA: Just! Looking for some . . . thing.

GIRL 2: You couldn't have sold all the coffee.

BARISTA: I traded it.

BOY: All of it?

GIRL 2: Who'd you trade with?

GIRL 1: Don't—

Explosions.

GIRL 1 whelps, ducks.

GIRL 2: Don't be a girl.

BOY: Who'd you trade with? Well?

GIRL 2: Whose side are you on?

Pause.

Ask her/him.

GIRL 1: Whose side are you on?

BARISTA: No one's!

BOY: I know whose side s/he's on.

BARISTA: No one's! I don't have sides. There are no sides.

BOY: What's that bottle? Who would trade him a bottle of drink for coffee?

GIRL 1: The rebels?

GIRL 2: It's an American bottle of drink!

BOY: Who would trade an American bottle of drink?

BARISTA: I'm on no one's side!

An explosion. Quite close. Lights flicker more.

GIRL 1: I see . . . I see a dragon's genitals swelling for the spring.

The BOY laughs.

GIRL 2: (*to BARISTA*) Why don't you go find us some more coffee?

The BOY laughs more.

GIRL 1: (*to GIRL 2*) I don't want coffee.

GIRL 2: You can drink their drink.

BOY: Yeah!

GIRL 2: Yeah, you can go find some more coffee. We can take care of your American drink.

BOY: Yeah!

BARISTA: I'm not—

BOY: Yeah! You are.

BARISTA: No, I'm not!

GIRL 2: C'mon, we want to taste what it tastes like.

BARISTA: You know what it tastes like.

GIRL 2: Do we?

BOY: Yeah!

GIRL 2: Don't be scared. I'm sure you won't have far to go.

The BOY and GIRL 2 grab the BARISTA.

BOY: Yeah!

An explosion.

BARISTA: (*to* GIRL 1) Help me!

The BOY *and* GIRL 2 *stare hard at* GIRL 1, *challenging her.*

GIRL 1: You're on the wrong side.

BARISTA: You think I chose a side? You think I chose a side? Look at you! You're fighting this war too. You are! Right now! Stop it! Let go! Stop it!

The BOY *and* GIRL 2 *push the* BARISTA *out.*

Pause.

GIRL 1: I see a scarecrow.

GIRL 2: You already saw a scarecrow.

The BOY *reaches for the bottle of tequila but* GIRL 1 *grabs it before he can.*

BOY: Hey! That's ours.

GIRL 1: I . . . want it.

GIRL 2: Whose side are you on?

GIRL 1: Whose side are you on?

They're frozen at this, standing around GIRL 1.

After a moment, GIRL 2 *breaks the silence:*

GIRL 2: You're so scared.

GIRL 1: Only because—!

BOY: Because of them?

GIRL 1: N— I knew them.

BOY: Was s/he nice?

GIRL 1: Doesn't matter.

GIRL 2: Were we right?

Pause.

An explosion.

BOY: This is boring.

GIRL 2: No it's not.

GIRL 1 starts to cry.

GIRL 2 motions to take the bottle, but GIRL 1 hits her with it. GIRL 2 falls to the ground. She is not dead but unable to sit back up, and remains so.

BOY: Hey!

Beat.

Absorbing what she just did, GIRL 1 *comes to her senses and threatens the* BOY *with the bottle.*

GIRL 1: I see a rat!

BOY: What?

GIRL 1: I see a tack sitting where I sat!

BOY: But—!

GIRL 1: Go on.

Beat.

BOY: Out there?

GIRL 1 *nods her head.*

The BOY *hesitates then runs outside as well.*

GIRL 1 *stares out the window after the* BOY, *holding the bottle and standing as if the coffee shop is the nation she just conquered. She watches the* BOY *running off into the hailstorm for a moment.*

Then she turns her head toward GIRL 2: *an afterthought of sympathy, remorse.*

Quick blackout.

FRANCES KONCAN
ZAHGIDIWIN/LOVE

Frances Koncan is an Indigenous artist of Anishinaabe descent. Her practice includes writing, directing, producing, music composition, and using social media to form friendships with celebrities. She holds an M.F.A. in Playwriting from the City University of New York Brooklyn College and a B.A. in Psychology from the University of Manitoba. Her work as a playwright includes *Little Red*, *How to Talk to Human Beings*, *The Dance-off of Conscious Uncoupling*, *zahgidiwin/love*, *Riot Resist Revolt Repeat*, and *Women of the Fur Trade*. Awards include the Winnipeg Arts Council On the Rise Award, the Manitoba Association of Playwrights Emerging Artist Award, and a REVEAL Indigenous Arts Award. Originally from Couchiching First Nation, she currently resides in Treaty 1 Territory in the city known as Winnipeg, where she lives alone with her dog Tucker.

zahgidiwin/love is a dark comedy about trauma, genocide, and decolonization amidst an era of Truth and Reconciliation. Using the collective culture of contemporary colonial Canada, the play is set across three time periods of Canadian history: a residential school in the '60s, a murderer's basement in the '90s, and a castle in the postapocalyptic future. Through a kaleidoscope of theatrical styles, the play explores the ramifications of trauma across generations, and searches for what a decolonized nation and decolonized theatre might look like.

zahgidiwin/love was first produced by Vault Projects, Winnipeg, on July 13, 2016.

* * *

NARRATOR: The Present, Chapter 1. A suburban basement in the 1990s.

A toilet flushes. A Heterosexual White Male (HWM) enters. He sits and rubs his belly like it's a fat, furry cat.

NAMID and Missing Girl 24601 (MG2) enter and stand behind him.

HWM: Come, my most useful possessions, and join me for dinner. I have prepared a great feast.

NAMID opens her mouth to speak, but is silenced.

MG2: Shh. Don't. It's not the right time. Wait until the flood comes.

NAMID: But he did not prepare the feast.

MG2: Shh! Sure he did! See, it's all right here. Mmm, feast.

(to HWM) Such a delicious feast made by a most magnanimous man!

NAMID: We prepared a feast. We: me and you, you and I. And I want credit for my work and equal pay.

MG2: But the flood will come soon and balance will be restored. Does it do any harm if we just let him take credit until then?

NAMID: We can't just wait for a flood to deus ex machina us out of captivity and back to our homes and families.

MG2: I don't think it's a deus ex machina if we're relying on it from the beginning.

NAMID: I don't think it's a deus ex machina if it isn't even real!

MG2: It is real. When the Supreme Queen's ungrateful daughter turns sixteen years old and enslaves her first mad, the deluge will begin and all oppression will be washed away.

NAMID: Dumb. Water doesn't wash away the past. There can be no healing until our oppressors acknowledge their crimes against my ancestors and—

MG2: You know that sort of talk makes me uncomfortable. Anyway, white people have it just as bad! Now, can we please eat? I want cake.

NAMID: Vanilla cake?

MG2: Rude.

HWM clears his throat.

HWM: I have asked you both to join me here tonight for this great feast I have prepared with my own two capable hands, which are very big, and you know what they say about men with big hands, ahahaha ahehehe haw haw haw . . .

NARRATOR: The man leans back in his chair and spreads his legs far apart, making sure everyone notices that he has a penis in there somewhere.

He slaps NAMID on the butt.

NAMID: Enough!

HWM screams.

330 | FRANCES KONCAN

MG2: Oh my goodness, are you okay?

He screams again and falls out of his chair.

NARRATOR: Up until this exact moment, the man has not heard a single word they have said. In fact, he has been unaware up until now that women are even capable of speaking, and I'm afraid the news comes as a great shock to him.

HWM: You can talk?!

NAMID: Of course we can talk.

MG2: Are you okay? Did you hurt yourself? Can I get you some tea?

HWM: I cannot believe I own not one talking woman but two. Two! Oh me, oh my, my goodness, my gracious, isn't this just the wow, wow, gosh, wow, gosh wow gosh! That is special. I've never kidnapped a woman who could talk before. Are there more of your kind?

NAMID: A few.

HWM: Holy moly. Shucks. Well. Help me up.

NARRATOR: The man extends both hands in to the air and squirms helplessly on the floor like a useless baby.

MG2 tries to grab his hand but NAMID slaps it away.

NAMID: First, say please.

HWM: Help me up.

NAMID: Say please!

HWM: Help me up!

NAMID: Saaay. Puuuuhleaze.

HWM: I said heeeeeeelllllllp meup.

NAMID: And I said you have to say please.

HWM: P . . . p . . . p . . . . p . . . . lice? Puh-loice. Puh-layce. Puh-leeee . . . aaaa . . . seeaah.

NAMID extends her hand and the man takes it. She pulls him halfway up.

NAMID: Why did you kidnap us?

HWM: Dunno. You seemed like an easy target.

MG2: What about me? My family will be looking for me!

HWM: Truuuue, but you're not blond. I'd be more worried if you were blond.

NAMID drops him back to the ground, hard.

HWM: Ow.

NAMID: Getting real sick of your shit.

MG2 helps HWM back into his chair.

Great. That's just great, Patty Hearst.

MG2: Being kidnapped is no excuse for bad manners.

HWM: Agreed. Truly, I have taught you well. Now, won't you poh-lease both join me for dinner. I have prepared a great feast.

Yvette Nolan is a playwright, dramaturg, and director. She has written several plays, including *Annie Mae's Movement*, BLADE, and *Job's Wife*. She has been writer-in-residence at Brandon University, Mount Royal College, and the Saskatoon Public Library, as well as playwright-in-residence at the National Arts Centre. Born in Saskatchewan to an Algonquin mother and an Irish immigrant father and raised in Manitoba, Yvette lived in the Yukon and Nova Scotia before moving to Toronto where she served as artistic director of Native Earth Performing Arts from 2003 to 2011.

Donna-Michelle St. Bernard is an emcee, playwright, and arts administrator. Her work has been recognized with a Siminovitch Prize nomination, SATAward nomination, the Herman Voaden Playwriting Award, the Enbridge playRites Award, a Dora Mavor Moore Award for Outstanding New Play, and two nominations for the Governor General's Literary Award for Drama. She is the current artistic director of New Harlem Productions. She is based in Toronto.

First edition: December 2020
Printed and bound in Canada by Imprimerie Gauvin, Gatineau

Jacket design by Kisscut Design
Jacket photo © Flügelwesen / photocase.com

202-269 Richmond St. W.
Toronto, ON
M5V 1X1

416.703.0013
info@playwrightscanada.com
www.playwrightscanada.com
@playcanpress